# Climate Change, Trade and Natural Disasters

# Climate Change, Trade and Natural Disasters

BISWAJIT CHATTERJEE
Professor of Economics
Jadavpur University, Kolkata

DEEP & DEEP PUBLICATIONS PVT. LTD.
F-159, Rajouri Garden, New Delhi - 110 027

CLIMATE CHANGE, TRADE AND NATURAL DISASTERS

ISBN 978-81-8450-363-0



Typeset by RAHUL COMPOSERS
358, Pocket-B, Phase-2, Sector-16B, Dwarka, New Delhi - 110 075

Printed in India at MAYUR ENTERPRISES
WZ Plot No. 3, Gujjar Market, Tihar Village, New Delhi - 110 018

Published by DEEP & DEEP PUBLICATIONS PVT. LTD.,
F-159, Rajouri Garden, New Delhi - 110 027 • Phone : 25435369, 25440916
E-mail : ddpbooks@yahoo.co.in • ddpubs@gmail.com
*Showroom :*
2/13, Ansari Road, Daryaganj, New Delhi - 110 002 • Telefax : 23245122

# Contents

# Preface

This is a collection of three essays on very important economic events of recent times: climate change, international trade and natural disasters. Although the scientific community has warned about the disastrous and damaging consequences of climate change and related aberrations on economic development, the events have increasingly attracted the attention of researchers and policy-makers in the domain of economics. In this monograph comprising three essays, an attempt has been made to review the major economic issues to bring into focus the choices and constraints faced by human race, particularly in the developing world to mitigate and combat the consequences of climate change and natural disasters. The implications of climate change for economic development of nations have been spelt out through the review of relevant literature in the first essay of the monograph. When open economy issues are included in the discourse on climate change, particularly in a globalised world, the link between international trade, climate change, technological change and scope for multilateral trade negotiations under the WTO have been reviewed critically in the second essay of the volume. The third and final essay of the volume portrays an analytical review of the link between climate change, nature and types of natural disasters, their macroeconomic impacts on growth, development and technological progress and the implications of disaster insurance to combat and mitigate the adverse effects of natural disasters which have been largely influenced by climatic variations. Each essay in the volume adds a large list of references to the literature on the subject and issues covered. While theoretical and policy researches in these areas have picked up in recent times, there is a lot that needs to be addressed. The policy response at both national and international levels have remained rather sluggish, because many of the choices and constraints are yet to be solved satisfactorily.

The discussions on climate change, disaster and trade-related measures combating their impact have been continuing for several years in recent times. Particularly in the context of development of a poor nation, the main focus of all these discussions in economics, has been to plan for the future development strategies in an uncertain and stochastic world. The resources available at the Planning and Development Unit of Jadavpur University and the support it provides, have enabled me to reflect and put together the diverse issues within the short contours of this monograph. During the Summer of 2010, I thank Jadavpur University for all the support and to the researchers and scholars of the Planning and Development Unit of the University for their kind cooperation and help, without implicating them for what are written. I am also thankful to Shri G.S. Bhatia of Deep and Deep Publications, New Delhi for bringing out the volume in an elegant manner.

BISWAJIT CHATTERJEE

# Introduction

The developmental concern following climate change assume importance in the context efforts to induce inclusive economic growth, poverty reduction and sustainable economic development over the long-run, and the adverse impacts of climate change often depend on sectors that are susceptible to climate fluctuations, such as agriculture, fisheries, forestry and tourism. Poorer countries are often less capable of adapting to the adverse impacts of climate change. There are two implications of the long-term consequences of climate change. The first is that the choice of the discount rate used to make comparisons of income losses across time is critical to assess the trade-offs between the nearer-term costs of mitigation and the longer-term losses from warming. Given that discounting takes place over many years, even relatively small differences in the discount rate can have a very large impact on such assessment. The second implication of the long-term analysis of climate change is high uncertainty and the relevant timeframe is measured in many decades, sometimes centuries. Available evidences indicate that some climate indicators are changing near the upper bound of the IPCC (2007) projection range. IPCC (2007) projected that a further warming of about 0.1 degrees Celsius per decade would be expected even if the concentrations of all GHGs had been kept constant at year 2000 levels. Continued greenhouse gas emissions at or above current rates would cause further warming and induce many changes in the global climate system. It is argued that setting a strong mitigation target and adopting a low carbon economic growth model is the only sustainable development path for developing countries. Going low-carbon is costly in the short-term, but the potential benefits could be huge in the long-run. As the financial needs to address climate change are large, global, and urgent, the challenge of responding to climate change presents itself as a unique opportunity for developing countries. Fairness and capacity concerns will argue for that the financing needs should be met primarily by developed countries. The two main channels are either the publicly funded programmes/channel or private channel (carbon markets) to deliver these needed mitigation and adaptation finance to developing countries. If no mitigation and adaptation actions are taken, climate change may not only threaten to unwind the development progress made so far, but could also impact development today and development prospects tomorrow.

In the simplified deterministic setting, the discount rate depends on preference-related parameters and the rate of growth of the global economy. When the discussions on the discount rate are extended to a stochastic setting, incorporating uncertainty in the model but still under a single-world framework, the discount rate is not uniquely determined if we account for risk while incorporating structural uncertainty. When we go beyond a single world approach to an asymmetric world where heterogeneity in preferences, income distribution and consumption goods are taken into account, the choice of the discount rate becomes flat-tailed. In case of discounting under certainty in a single world, both ethical judgments and empirical information that assess preference parameters from observed behaviour, are often used sometimes in combination. As both adaptation and mitigation efforts are continuously re-evaluated in the light of new information and findings, adopting a composite policy involving both adaptation and mitigation may be more effective. Creating an environment in which economic development can take place is seemed as another form of insurance since it will enable people who are currently vulnerable to the climate change to diversify their economic activities and thereby become more robust and sustainable in the face of climate challenges.

Policy-makers concerned about inter-generational inequality probably would apply a lower "ethical" rate of pure time preference in climate risk assessments to evaluate benefits received by future generations, so as to not trivialize these benefits relative to current costs. On the other hand, if the consumption growth rate per capita actually would fall over time with the threat of climate change, it could lead to a lower discount rate. Especially if we project global consumption growth rates using population weights instead of GDP weights, the future negative effects of global warming on the growth of fast-growing populous developing economies would reduce the overall global growth rate even more compared to the GDP-weighted methodology. This could lead to an even lower discount rate and a stronger policy implication for immediate actions on climate change. The threat to long-term sustainability of the growth process of the developing countries trying to catch-up with the advanced nations of today, is serious and so also the threat to livelihood security of the vast majority of poor and vulnerable sections of the population who are concentrated in these developing countries of Asia, Africa and Latin America. The first essay in the volume tries to address the above issues.

Although the impacts of climate change are specific to location and to the level of development, most sectors of the global economy are expected to be affected and these impacts will often have implications for trade. Three trade-related areas are considered to be particularly vulnerable to climate change: *Agriculture, Tourism, and trade infrastructure and routes*. The phenomenal expansion in global trade over recent decades and the concern for climate change induced threat to the sustainability of growth process in developed and developing countries has raised questions about the effect of international trade on climate change, which are discussed in detail in the second essay of the volume. There are three main ways in which trade openness could affect the amount of emissions, namely, the scale, composition and technique effects. The *scale effect* refers to the expansion of economic activity arising from trade opening, and its effect on greenhouse gas emissions. This increased level of economic activity will require greater energy use and will therefore lead to higher levels of greenhouse gas emissions. The *composition effect* describes the way that trade opening changes the structure of a country's production in response to changes in relative prices, and the consequences of this on emission levels. The effect on a country's greenhouse gas emissions will depend on whether a country has a comparative advantage in emission-intensive sectors and whether these sectors are expanding or contracting. Finally, the *technique effect* refers to improvements in the methods by which goods and services are produced, so that the emission intensity of output is reduced. This is the principal way in which trade opening can help mitigate climate change.

Most econometric studies suggested that more open trade would be likely to increase $CO_2$ emissions, as the scale effect would tend to dominate the technique and composition effects. Some studies, however, suggested that there might be differences in impact on emissions between developed and developing countries, with improvement being observed in OECD countries and deterioration in developing countries. Although many developed countries now require environmental assessments of any trade agreements that they had entered into, these assessments would tend to focus on national rather than cross-border or global pollutants. A few of these assessments had raised concerns about the possible increase in greenhouse gas emissions from increased transport activity, although a detailed quantitative analysis of the effects on emission levels of increased transportation is few. Some studies also tried to account for the contribution of international trade to $CO_2$ emissions. Since consumption, by definition, involves trade (consumption = production + imports – exports), it is necessary to estimate the $CO_2$ emissions "embodied" in trade. However, these estimates do not imply that halting international trade would eliminate 21.5 per cent of greenhouse gas emissions, since domestic products would take the place of imported products.

There have been significant overlaps between climate change and trade policies and intense negotiations at different international fora have taken place over the implications of multilateral interventions. In the Marrakesh Agreement establishing the WTO, members highlighted a clear link between sustainable development and trade opening in order to ensure that market opening goes hand in hand with environmental and social objectives. In the Doha Round of negotiations, members went further in their pledge to pursue a sustainable development path by launching the first-ever multilateral trade and environment negotiations. Decisions in these multilateral regimes—but also more broadly in regional, bilateral and national arenas—are likely to greatly influence the future of both international trade and the global climate. The use of trade-related measures has so far been eschewed under the UNFCCC or Kyoto Protocol, even if they have been used in other multilateral environmental agreements, such as the Montreal Protocol for the Protection of the Ozone Layer. Moreover, climate negotiators have typically avoided trade-related issues, preferring to defer these issues to the WTO. In a similar vein, the WTO has been very cautious in addressing climate change, often highlighting that such issues are more suitably decided within the climate change regime.

There appear to be two likely effects of climate change on international trade. First, climate change may alter countries' comparative advantages and lead to shifts in the pattern of international trade, particularly in those countries whose comparative advantage stems from climatic or geophysical reasons. Countries or regions that are more reliant on agriculture may experience a reduction in exports if future warming and more frequent extreme weather events result in a reduction in crop yields. Warming as such need not always produce negative impacts on exports, since it may succeed in increasing agricultural yields in other regions. These climate change effects will not necessarily be confined to trade in merchandise goods but might extend to trade in services as well.

The second most important issue pertaining to the climate change literature has been the link between climate change and natural disasters, and the impacts of such catastrophic events on economic growth, measurement of risks, and insurance against such disasters. The third and final essay of the volume addresses these issues. The theoretical and empirical analysis of the impact of natural disasters on poverty and vulnerability of the affected people in different parts of the globe, the uncertainty and risk associated with such disaster consequences and the estimation of losses due to such events, nature of insurance markets to mitigate the losses or damages due to disaster, and the policy interventions by national governments and the international aid inflows and associated problems of such aid management have been discussed in this essay. It is argued that the complex issues of insuring against catastrophic events be left not only to private players in insurance markets, particularly in developing countries like India where such markets are not well-developed, explicit strategy by the government needs to be devised to cope with the losses that affect the lives and fortunes of the people, and sustain the process of economic development of such nations.

BISWAJIT CHATTERJEE

# 1

# Climate Change and Challenges for Development

Climate change is increasingly regarded not only as an environmental or intergenerational sustainability issue but also as a development concern. Responding to climate change is required for inclusive economic growth, poverty reduction, and development over the long-run. The effects of climate change are not homogenous : they affect the poorest more quickly and more deeply than the rich nations. The impacts of climate change vary depending on where one lives. Climate change imposes asymmetric impacts not only on economic development but also on human development. If we exclude extreme consequences of warming, such as the catastrophic events that are likely to leave every country and virtually every person worse-off, climate change affects different regions and different groups of people differently. Some impacts could be beneficial in some locations for some time with a few degrees of warming, but most impacts are expected to be adverse (UNDP, 2007). Poor developing countries are particularly vulnerable to the adverse impacts of climate change because many of these economies depend on sectors that are susceptible to climate fluctuations, such as agriculture, fisheries, forestry and tourism. Poorer countries are also less capable of adapting to the adverse impacts of climate change. The poorest countries and people are suffering the most in terms of the effects of climate change, and this pattern is likely to persist in the future. If this pattern does persist, climate change will hurt economic growth, drive income divergence and deepen global inequalities. The exposure of the poor to extreme weather risks is heavily skewed towards developing countries.

The economics of climate change is often framed as a choice between two possible scenarios. In scenario I, we may choose to live in a world where we do nothing now to mitigate climate change, but in the future will have to suffer income losses from the damages of warming. In the scenario II, we may choose to live in a world where those future income losses are avoided, but at the expense of taking costly action starting now or very soon to mitigate climate change, which implies cuts in GDP growth in the short-run. In this second scenario, avoided future losses from climate change are benefits while current incomes foregone to receive those future benefits are costs. This is how cost-benefit analysis of climate change is typically described. Such an analysis relates climate change to trade-offs across generations, because it is viewed as a very long-term challenge. There are two important implications of considering climate change as a very long-term issue. The first is that the choice of the discount rate used to make comparisons of income losses across time is critical to assess the trade-offs between the nearer-term costs of mitigation and the longer-term losses from warming. Given that discounting takes place over many years, even relatively small differences in the discount rate can have a very large impact on this assessment. The second implication of the long-term analysis of climate change is high uncertainty. The relevant timeframe is measured in many decades, sometimes centuries. We only need to have in mind how the world was in 1908 to realize how much can change over the course of a century. The long-term nature of climate change, coupled with the complexity of climate systems, implies that while we know that the earth is warming, we do not know how fast and how far the implications from this warming will be with certainty. Catastrophic outcomes that can change the world in fundamental ways—like a new ice age or increases in sea levels by twenty meters—while unlikely in the short-run, are not impossible within a timeframe of one to two centuries. This implies, in turn, that a deterministic setting may be incomplete for analyzing climate change. Thus, it is worthwhile to explicitly consider risk and uncertainty when determining the amount of income losses and the value of the discount rate.

The long-term losses from global warming typically underestimate damages from climate change once natural assets that are not captured by national accounts—like the existence value for certain species or ecosystems—are factored in. But such a simplified and ultra-stylized single world analysis is grossly inadequate to analyze the challenge of climate change. It is important to note the asymmetries that exist in the world and thus the impact of climate change on income distributions. Income distributions intersect with climate change at two levels: first, in terms of the causes of climate change (emissions of greenhouse gases) and second, in terms of the effects of climate change. In the first case, asymmetries in contributions to the current stocks of greenhouse gases are intimately linked to differences across countries in the accumulation of global income over time. Today's richest countries have the overwhelming responsibility for the accumulated stocks of greenhouse gases in the atmosphere. If we look at the flows of emissions, rich countries remain important emitters, but a few large developing countries have also started to contribute significantly to such emissions. There exists a third group of countries that have not contributed much, either historically or now, and they have the lowest shares of today's world income. In so far as distribution of income across persons, the losses of income that are predicted if mitigation is taken up will fall on some people more than others. For example, strong mitigation measures may hurt economies that are heavily dependent on fossil fuels and within countries, many people that work in or are dependent on emission intensive activities may be economically displaced. Of course, these future income distributional issues linked with emissions could be managed if appropriate transfer mechanisms are evolved. If we exclude extreme consequences of warming, such as the catastrophic events that are likely to leave every country and virtually every person worse-off, climate change affects different regions and different groups of people differently. Some regions in the North may even benefit from warmer temperatures and increased rainfall. But the effects in tropical regions are and will be overwhelmingly negative. The poorest countries and people are suffering the most in terms of the effects of climate change, and this pattern is likely to persist in the future. If this pattern does persist, climate change will drive income divergence and deepen global inequalities.

The plan of the present paper is as follows. Section I summarises the results of different studies about climate change and the evidences that are available to suggest long-term implications of development following climate change. Section II reviews the implications for cost benefit analysis of the valuation of catastrophic losses that threaten development process following climate change. Section III discusses the implications of climate change for the economic development of nations in general and developing countries in particular, especially in respect of poverty among the vulnerable groups in developing world. Section IV summarises the main conclusions.

## SECTION I

## EVIDENCES

Global efforts to mitigate climate change have been guided by updated climate change evidences. IPCC (2007) reports numerous observed long-term changes in climate. These include changes in arctic temperatures and ice, widespread changes in precipitation amounts, ocean salinity, wind patterns and extreme weather events including droughts, heavy precipitation, heat waves and intense tropical cyclones. From the observations of increases in global average air and ocean temperatures, widespread melting of snow and ice, and rising global average sea level, warming of the climate system is evident. Since the publication of the latest report by IPCC (2007), new evidence from physical climate science has also become available to indicate that some climate indicators are changing near the upper bound of the IPCC (2007) projection range. Some aspects of climate change are progressing faster than was previously thought. For example, Richardson *et al.* (2009) has shown sea level rises at greater rates than indicated by IPCC (2007). The rate of sea-level rise has increased in the period from 1993 to the present, rising near the upper bound of the IPCC (2007) projections. Pfeffer *et al.* (2008) predict a best guess of about 0.8 meters sea level rise by 2100. Grinsted *et al.* (2009) use a moderate climate change scenario (IPCC's A1B emission scenario) to project a range of 0.9 to 1.3 meters of sea level rise in 2090 to 2100. Dahl-Jensen *et al.* (2009) use the new data of the increasing loss of mass from glaciers, ice caps and the Greenland and Antarctic ice sheets to conclude an alarming prediction of global mean sea level rise of 1 meter by the end of 21st century (2090-99) compared to the end of 20th century (1980-1999), which almost doubles the IPCC projection made in 2007 (at a range of 0.18 to 0.59 meter rise for the 120-year period). Domingues *et al.* (2008) and Church *et al.* (2009) report updated trends in ocean heat content and surface ocean temperature. Both studies find the ocean has warmed significantly in recent years. Domingues *et al.* (2008) plot a linear trend of global ocean heat content over the period of 1961-2003 based on updated global ocean heat content data. The new linear trend is 50 percent steeper than the linear trend previous reported by IPCC (2007) which implies a higher rate of multi-decadal warming .

There exists a large empirical literature studying the direct relationship between climatic shocks and economic growth. For example, the IMF (2003) finds that large-scale natural disasters have occurred on average once every 20 years in least developed countries (LDCs) over the 1977-2001 period, with an average impact on GDP ranging from -2.7 percent to -5.8 percent in the most recent (1997-2001) period. Since climate change may increase the frequency and severity of natural disasters, the IMF study suggests that climate change could strongly affect growth in developing countries, in the absence of mitigation or adaptation policies. Dell, Jones and Olken (2008) compare individual country's historical temperature and precipitation data with historical growth data from 1950 to 2003 and find higher temperature substantially reduce economic growth in poor countries but have little effect in rich countries. In poorer countries, they estimate that a 1 degree Celsius rise in temperature in a given year reduces economic growth in that year by about 1.1 percentage points. In a follow-up study, Dell, Jones and Olken (2009) use 12-country municipal data to find a negative within-country relationship between income and temperature, with a 1 degree Celsius rise in temperature associated with a 1.2-1.9 percent decline in municipal per-capita income.

The climate-development relationship is complex. Climate change could be a 'threat multiplier' that makes existing development challenges more complex and intractable (Brown and Crawford, 2009). There have been research linking climate change to agriculture (Cline, 2007), to food security (Batissi and Naylor 2009, Nellemann *et al.*, 2009), to water scarcity (Böhner and Lehmkuhl, 2005, Thompson and others, 2002), to health (IPCC 2007), and to conflict (Brown and Crawford, 2009), all of which have direct and indirect effects on economic activity. Cline (2007) predicts that developing countries will suffer an average 10–25 percent decline in agricultural productivity by the 2080s, assuming 'business as usual', and ignoring carbon fertilization. Declines in agriculture productivity will be much steeper in some countries. For example, India may face a decline of 30–40 per cent of agriculture productivity, Sudan a 56 per cent drop, and Senegal a 52 per cent fall. Batissi and Naylor (2009) exhibit that it is very likely (greater than 90 percent in probability) that the tropics and subtropics will experience unprecedented seasonal (summer) heat by the end of the century. Thus many developing countries in the regions could experience significant losses of agriculture productivity. Using historical data on seasonal heat and crop yields, the authors illustrates the damage extreme seasonal heat may cause to regional and global food security. Nellemann *et al.* (2009) warn that up to 25 percent of the world food production may be "lost", under a business-as-usual scenario, during the 21st century as a result of climate change, water scarcity and land degradation. Therefore, it is very likely to have an even more volatile and escalating food prices and threaten the food security in many climate-vulnerable developing countries. For example, severe heat in the summer of 2003 resulted in a drop in maize yields by 36 percent in Italy and by 30 percent in France; a prolonged hot summer of 1972 caused a 13 percent decline in grain production in the former USSR.

IFPRI (2009) estimates that in some developing countries some crop yields in 2050 could be only half of their 2000 levels due to the effects of climate change, and under a business-as-usual scenario. Irrigation may not help as climate change is likely to hit irrigated systems harder. South Asia, the world's most heavily populated region, looks more vulnerable: IFPRI forecasts a possible 50 percent fall in its wheat yield by 2050 with no $CO_2$ fertilization effect (higher $CO_2$ concentrations in the atmosphere could help "fertilize" plant growth and increase crop yields) compared to 1990. The negative effects of climate change on crop production are especially significant in Sub-Saharan Africa and South Asia between 2000 and 2050. In South Asia, climate change is projected to result in a 14-percent decline in rice production relative to the no–climate-change scenario, a 44 to 49 percent decline in wheat production, and a 9 to 19 percent fall in maize production (with no $CO_2$ fertilization effect). In Sub-Saharan Africa, the rice, wheat, and maize production declines with climate change are 15 percent, 34 percent, and 10 percent (with no $CO_2$ fertilization effect), respectively (IFPRI, 2009). These estimates are all under a business as usual scenario. IFPRI, (2009) forecasts that between 2000 and 2050 climate change could result in additional price increases for agricultural crops: 32 to 37 percent for rice, 52 to 55 percent for maize, 94 to 111 percent for wheat, and 11 to 14 percent for soybeans (with no $CO_2$ fertilization effect). There is also the likely impact of climate change on health. The IPCC (2007) projects that climate change related exposures are likely to affect the health status of millions of people, particularly those with low adaptive capacity. This is likely to happen through increases in malnutrition and consequent disorders; increased injury, disease, and death due to heat waves, floods, storms, fires, and droughts; the increased burden of diarrhoeal disease; the mixed effects on the range and transmission potential of malaria in Africa; and increased frequency of cardio-respiratory diseases due to higher concentrations of ground level ozone related to climate change. IFPRI (2009) finds that calorie availability throughout the developing world in 2050 is forecasted to be lower not only than in the no–climate-change scenario but also compared to 2000 levels (under a business as usual scenario). For the average consumer in a developing country, the decline is 7 percent relative to 2000 (with no $CO_2$ fertilization) if no action is taken to mitigate climate change. By 2050, the decline in calorie availability will increase child malnutrition by 20 percent (with no $CO_2$ fertilization effect) relative to a world with no climate change.

Climate change will hit some countries harder than others. ADB (2009) finds global warming under a business as usual scenario is likely to cause rice yield potential to decline by up to 50 percent on average by 2100 compared to 1990 in Indonesia, Philippines, Thailand, and Vietnam. For these four countries, the potential economic cost of inaction each year could equal a loss of 6.7 percent of their combined gross domestic product by 2100, more than twice the world average loss. Global warming could increase the number of deaths from heat-related cardiovascular and respiratory diseases relative to the estimated number of deaths from these diseases without climate change by as much as 2.9 percent and 12.4 percent by 2050 and 9.2 percent and 20.4 percent by 2100 in the four countries. The economic development in some poor Asian and African countries is also threatened by increasingly severe water scarcity which is associated with the retreat of glaciers. Thompson *et al.* (2002) report tropical glaciers in Africa have decreased by 60 to 70 percent since the early 1900s. According to Böhner and Lehmkuhl (2005), up to 80 percent of the glaciated area in Central and High Asia may be lost within this century with rising temperatures. Climate-induced conflicts may also emerge through several channels (Brown and Crawford, 2009). For example, deteriorating water scarcity may lead to increasing competition between different sectors, different communities and different countries. Increasingly unpredictable weather patterns could result in reductions in crop yields which will push food prices higher and fuel social tensions. Sea level rise, increased natural disasters and the shrinking viable agricultural land may cause large-scale and destabilizing forced migration. Combined with poor governance and existing ethnic division, the above stresses may tip fragile states towards socioeconomic and political collapse.

Sokolov *et al.* (2009) report new projections of surface temperature based on the MIT Integrated Global System Model. Compared to their year 2003 projection of 2.4 degrees Celsius warming, the new study projects a median probability of surface warming of 5.2 degrees Celsius in 2091 to 2100, with a 90 percent probability range of 3.5 to 7.4 degrees. Their stronger warming result is quite robust. Several factors contribute to the stronger warming projection, among which is an updated economic model of GDP growth projection that eliminate many low emission scenarios used in the earlier study.

IPCC (2007) projects that a further warming of about 0.1 degrees Celsius per decade would be expected even if the concentrations of all GHGs had been kept constant at year 2000 levels. Continued greenhouse gas emissions at or above current rates would cause further warming and induce many changes in the global climate system. Plattner (2009) and Solomon *et al.* (2009) find some daunting evidence that climate change may be irreversible for long time. Their studies suggest that even we cut greenhouse gas emissions to zero today it will take more than 1000 years for the global average surface temperature to drop. In 1996 the European Union set the goal of limiting warming to 2 degrees Celsius (3.6 Fahrenheit) above pre-industrial levels. In the latest La Quilla G8 summit, world leaders also agreed a goal of limiting global warming to 2 degrees Celsius. Drawing on the latest scientific, economic and social evidence on climate change, Richardson *et al.* (2009) emphasizes a warming beyond 2 degrees is dangerous and are likely to cause major societal and environmental disruptions through the rest of the century and beyond. However, even with the most and stringent emission reduction action to achieve peak emissions in 2015, it is still likely to overshoot our current temperature targets of 2 degrees Celsius. If global emissions climb until 2025, the projected peak median temperature will rise to 2.5 degrees Celsius; if global emissions peak in 2035, the projected median temperature will be as high as 3 degrees Celsius. It may be noted that the long-term nature of climate change, coupled with the complexity of climate systems, implies that while we know that climate is changing, we do not know how fast and how far the implications from this change will be with certainty. The greater are uncertainties, the greater is the risk of waiting. As Quiggin (2008) concludes that "the more uncertain we are about the outcomes, the more certain we should be about the need to take action that reduces the rate of climate change."

McKinsey (2009), one of the latest reports adopting the bottom-up approach to estimate the global emission mitigation potential, look at mitigation potential across 10 sectors (power, petroleum and gas, cement, iron and steel, chemicals, other industry, transport, buildings, waste, forestry, and agriculture). Identifying all the technical mitigation measures costing less than 60 per tonne of $CO_2$ equivalent (see Figure 5), McKinsey

(2009) finds a global mitigation potential of 38 Gt $CO_2$ equivalent in 2030, which will bring global emissions to 32 Gt $CO_2$ equivalent. This is a 55 percent cut compared with the business-as-usual (BAU) scenario in 2030 (70 Gt $CO_2$ equivalent), 30 percent emission cut from 2005 global emission levels (46 Gt $CO_2$ equivalent), and 11 percent emission cut from 1990 levels (36 Gt $CO_2$ equivalent). The McKinsey estimate on global mitigation potential by 2030 is comparable to the IPCC (2007) bottom-up estimate for the high carbon price case ($100 per tonne of $CO_2$ equivalent). Energy efficiency and low carbon technology has been developing rapidly over the last two years, but meanwhile there had been an upward revision on global economic growth, especially on developing countries' growth projections. These two factors have opposite effect on the estimate of global mitigation potential.

According to McKinsey (2009), adopting technical mitigation measures to cut global emissions to 32 Gt $CO_2$ equivalent by 2030 is consistent with the long-term 450 parts per million (ppm) concentration path peaking at 510 ppm. To limit global warming to 2 degrees Celsius above pre-industrial levels, a deeper emission cut is needed. Another 9 Gt $CO_2$ equivalent emissions cut are required from more expensive technical measures and behaviour changes so that global emissions can be brought down to 23 Gt $CO_2$ equivalent a year by 2030, which is consistent with the long term 400 ppm concentration path peaking at 480 ppm. The 400 ppm atmospheric concentration pathway, according to McKinsey (2009), is likely to limit global warming to 2 degrees Celsius.This 50 percent global emission reduction by 2030 compared to 2005 levels (47 Gt $CO_2$ equivalent compared to BAU) will be a very challenging target.It is worthy to note that the McKinsey mitigation potential estimate of 38 Gt $CO_2$ equivalent, however, has already been based on very aggressive assumptions5 made by McKinsey (2009) in terms of strong and wide implementation of energy efficiency and low-carbon technologies across sectors and across regions. In other words, this mitigation potential represents a very optimistic emission reduction the world can realize if all the affordable energy efficiency and low-carbon technology opportunities are captured fully. Therefore the emission cut of 47 Gt $CO_2$ equivalent needed to limit global warming to 2 degrees Celsius will be even harder to achieve.

Environmental Kuznets Curves (EKCs) have been used by some developing countries to argue that their on-going economic growth will automatically erase environmental degradation so that they can choose to grow first and clean up later. But the EKCs have been proved largely a myth, and especially there is no clear-cut evidence to support the EKCs for carbon emissions in non-OECD countries (Stern, 2004; Marzio, Alessandro and Francesco, 2006). Instead, some experts have argued that setting a strong mitigation target and adopting a low carbon economic growth model is the only sustainable development path for developing countries (Stern, 2009). Going low-carbon is costly in the short-term, but the potential benefits could be huge in the long-run. For example, developing renewable energy requires significant fixed investment but could reduce a country's dependence on imported fossil fuels. Energy efficiency imposes an upfront expense but can help consumers and business saving energy costs for the long term. Low-carbon technologies are expensive to develop and put to use but will create new jobs and new sources of growth. The power, transport, building and industrial sectors, in particular, have been identified to have significant potential to benefit from low carbon technology and for emission cuts (Tomlinson, 2009). For some developing countries, going low carbon will even give them some comparative advantages because of their ample sources of renewable energy. The global market for low carbon technology goods and services has been growing rapidly due to the increasing demand for low carbon and energy efficiency goods and services. Innovas (2009) estimates that the global low carbon and environmental goods and services (LCEGS) market is worth about $4.65 trillion for 2007/2008, growing by 4 percent and projected to continue to grow. Traditional environmental activities account for 22 percent of the total LCEGS, renewable energy for 31 percent and the emerging low carbon for almost half of the global LCEGS market. The largest LCEGS by market value include alternative fuels, 19 percent (emerging low carbon sector), building technologies, 13 percent (emerging low carbon sector), wind power, 12 percent (renewable energy sector) and alternative fuels for vehicles, 11 percent (emerging low carbon sector). For the year 2007/2008, the renewable energy sector grows slightly faster than the other two sectors. Geographically, Asia occupies 38 percent, Europe 27 percent, and the Americas 30 percent of the global LCEGS market in 2007/ 2008. Among which are two fast growing developing economies China and India, accounting for 13.5 and 6.3 percent of the global market share. The $4.65 trillion global LCEGS market will create new demand for technologies, goods and services that will allow countries across the world to make the transition to a low carbon economy. New jobs will be created, and new business and profit opportunities will also emerge for well positioned business and companies. The Carbon Trust (2008) reports that a company that is well positioned and pro-active could increase its value by up to 80 percent by making the transition to low carbon based activities and markets. Innovas (2009) estimates in the UK today, there are about 881,000 jobs in the LCEGS sector and nearly half of them are in the emerging low carbon sector. It projects that this number will grow as UK take further actions to transit its economy to a low carbon one. According to Renner, Sweeney and Kubit (2008), the renewable energy sector of China is valued at nearly U$17 billion and employs almost 1 million workers in 2007, including 600,000 in solar thermal, 266,000 in biomass generation, 55,000 in solar photovoltaics (PV) and 22,200 in wind power. However, we cannot just wait for businesses and households to become ready and economically motivated enough to adopt low carbon production and consumption patterns. The public policy that guides, supports and creates incentives, therefore, appears to be critical as of now. A low carbon growth model is new for both developing and developed countries. Ironically, there have not been many developed-country role models exhibiting the low-carbon economic growth path is not only feasible but also efficient and desirable. Major developed economies have only started to take actions and transit their economies to low carbon ones.

There have been various studies to estimate the financing needed by developing countries for mitigation and adaption. UNFCCC (2008) estimates that additional mitigation investment and financial flows needed to cut global emission by more than 30 Gt $CO_2$ equivalent is $200 to $210 billion per year by 2030, and over half of the additional global investment and financial flows in mitigation would be needed in developing countries. The estimates have been suggested to be revised up because of higher projected capital costs in the energy sector (UNFCCC, 2008). McKinsey (2009) estimates that the global mitigation cost would be around €200 to €350 billion annually by 2030 based on its most optimistic set of assumptions ("the most economically rational abatement opportunities are pursued to their full potential"). The total upfront investment in abatement measures needed would be €530 billion in 2020 per year or €810 billion per year in 2030—incremental to business-as-usual (BAU) investments. McKinsey (2009) estimates that close to 60 percent of the total investments will be needed in developing countries, which is about €320 billion per year in 2020 and €490 billion per year in 2030. The estimate for adaptation financing is subject to high uncertainty and varies from study to study.

UNDP (2007) estimates the new and additional finance needed for adaptation in developing countries to protect the poor and MDG results is around $86 billion a year by 2015, representing about 0.2 percent of developed countries' GDP in 2015. World Bank (2006) estimate an amount of $10-40 billion a year by 2020 is needed to finance adaptation in developing countries. Stern *et al.* (2007) estimate an amount of $4-37 billion a year for climate proof investment on all adaptation-related activities in developing countries. Oxfam International (2007) estimated that adaptation will cost more than $50 billion annually in developing countries, and this amount has to be financed by additional and new sources. UNFCCC (2008) estimates the investment and capital flows needed for adaptation activities in developing countries in 2030 is about $28-58 billion a year.

Developing countries also speak out how much financing they need from developed countries. For example, the current G-77 and China proposal requests Annex I Parties contribute 0.5 to 1 percent of their Gross National Product (GNP), in addition to their existing ODA commitments, to mitigation, adaptation, technology transfer and capacity development activities, which could amount to some amount between $200 billion and $400 billion a year.

As the financial needs to address climate change are large, global, and urgent, the challenge of responding to climate change presents itself as a unique opportunity for developing countries. Fairness and capacity concerns will argue for that the financing needs should be met primarily by developed countries. The two main channels are either the publicly funded programmes/channel or private channel (carbon markets) to deliver these needed mitigation and adaptation finance to developing countries. Public funding for mitigation and adaptation in developing countries includes official development assistance (ODA) and the public funding provided under the Convention's financial mechanism, which is additional to the traditional ODA funding. In 2008, total net ODA from OECD's Development Assistance Committee (DAC) members is amounted to $114 billion (in 2007 prices) and at the highest level ever. Levina (2007), in a rough analysis on the categories of ODA-funded activities by OECD DAC countries from 2000 to 2005, suggests that about 30-40 percent of ODA is sensitive to climate risks and around 60 percent of overall ODA could be relevant to adaptive capacity and adaptation.

## Section II

## CHOICE OF DISCOUNT RATE

The phenomenon of climate change has influenced the development planner's task of valuation of risk which is an essential ingredient of choosing an optimal mitigation strategy for economic development. The problem boils down to the choice of the appropriate discount rate in face of uncertainty that climate change poses. In the realm of development policy social cost-benefit analysis is crucial in understanding the damages that currently are visible and the future losses that can be surmised in the face of uncertainties involved. If no mitigation and adaptation action is taken, climate change may not only threaten to unwind the development progress hardly made so far but also impact development today and development prospects tomorrow. Climate and development are closely related. There has been a rich and often heated debate on discounting rate to be chosen in view of the uncertainties unleashed by climate change. In the simplified deterministic setting, the discount rate depends on preference-related parameters and the rate of growth of the global economy. When we extend the discussions on the discount rate to a stochastic setting, incorporating uncertainty in the model but still under a single-world framework, the discount rate is not uniquely determined if we account for risk while incorporating structural uncertainty. When we go beyond a single world approach to an asymmetric world where heterogeneity in preferences, income distribution and consumption goods are taken into consideration, the choice of the discount rate becomes flat-tailed. In case of discounting under certainty in a single world, both ethical judgments and empirical information that assess preference parameters from observed behaviour are often used, sometimes in combination. Under strong assumptions and simplifications, a global social discount rate is given by :

$$r = \rho + \eta . g \qquad (1)$$

These strong assumptions include: the overall objective is assumed to be to maximize a social welfare function which is expressed as the integral across all households and all time of the utility of households; the utility is additively separable across time; the only determinant of utility is consumption at each instant; there is one representative household and the utility function is unchanging over time; utility is assumed to take a constant elasticity-of-substitution functional form. Equation (1) is the Ramsey formula for the social discount rate where r is the social discount rate and it is used to discount consumption; ρ is the pure time preference rate, and it is used to discount utility; η is the elasticity of marginal utility of consumption, measuring the relative curvature of the utility function, and g is the growth rate of consumption per capita. In the context of the single-world analysis under certainty, the issue is one of "consumption smoothing", and the debate is centered on the choices for the preference-related parameters of the discount rate: the rate of pure time preference (ρ) and the elasticity of marginal utility with respect to consumption (η).

From an individual's perspective, ρ measures "impatience". Since people in general prefer deriving utility today rather than tomorrow, it is usually assumed that the rate of pure time preference is positive—the higher the value of ρ, the more we disçount the future. A positive ρ means that the utility (or welfare) of future generations are valued less or "discounted" compared to the utility of present generations—the higher the value of ρ, the more we discount future generations' welfare. This principle of universalizability, meaning all generations should be treated alike, is proposed in the literature by Pigou (1932), Ramsey (1928), Harrod (1948), Koopmans (1965), Solow (1974), and Stern (2007), to argue for a low ρ close to zero. Stern's value of 0.1% is derived from the probability of human extinction given some catastrophic event. However, other authors like Arrow (1995), and Nordhaus (2007), argue that the implications of a close-to-zero rate of pure time preference in standard savings and investment models is inconsistent with plausible and observed savings behaviour. The generalized conditions of the Ramsey equation, 1/η, measures the inter-temporal elasticity of substitution while its reciprocal, η, also measures the coefficient of relative risk aversion. In calibrating a growth model, ρ and η cannot be chosen independently, because r and g are given, so the values of ρ and η are interdependent requiring their joint determination. When the analysis is extended to include uncertainty, there are two issues : (a) discounting under risk, that is, when the parameters describing the probabilistic behaviour of the growth rate of consumption per capita g are assumed to be known with certainty, and (b) the effects of structural uncertainty on discounting when the parameters describing the probabilistic distribution of g are, themselves, unknown. Weitzman (1998, and 1999) suggested that uncertainty reflected in future discount rates would result in a declining certainty-equivalent social discount rate over time and it may be essential to incorporate such a declining certainty-equivalent discount rate into any cost-benefit analysis of long-term environmental projects. According to Weitzman (1998), interest rates under uncertainty do not aggregate arithmetically into a certainty-equivalent interest rate. Instead we should average the probabilistic discount factors, not the likely future discount rates. If there is a subjective probability $p_i$ that the future discount rate $r_i$ is the correct rate to use, then the effective discount rate for time t will be:

$$r(t) = -\frac{\log \sum p_t e^{-r_i t}}{t} \quad (2)$$

This effective discount rate declines monotonically over time from the expected interest rate $r(0) = \sum p_i r_i$ to an asymptotic limit of $r(\infty) = \min\{r_i\}$. If we assume 10 potential future discount rate scenarios, and each scenario has an equal probability: p1 = p2 = ...= p10 = 0.1, the numerical example shows that the discount rate for the current year will be 5.46 percent, but it slides fast with time. For the period 10 years from the present, the certainty-equivalent discount rate drops to 5.09 percent; for the period 50 years from the present, the certainty-equivalent discount rate lowers to 3.75 percent, and for the period 100 years from now, the discount rate declines further to 2.84 percent and then to 2.08 percent for the period 200 years from the present. Weitzman (1999) concludes in the limit, as t goes to infinity, the discount rate converges to the lowest possible interest rate. Weitzman (2001) argued that even if each individual's discount rate is certain and held constant over time, the certainty-equivalent social discount rate will follow a Gamma distribution and decline over time because of the wide spread differences of opinion on what interest rate to use to discount over time. Weitzman (2007a) modeled two distinct interest rates by making the growth rate of consumption per capita g a random variable, normally distributed with mean μ and standard deviation σ (both known with certainty). He argued that all the uncertainty is captured in the path of g. Such an uncertainty will lead to a lower social discount rate than the one derived from the simple deterministic Ramsey model.

$$g \sim N(\mu, \acute{o}) \quad (3)$$

The expected marginal utility (EMU) of one additional sure unit of consumption derived from the model looks like:

$$EMU = e^{-\rho-\eta\mu+\frac{1}{2}\eta^2\sigma^2} \quad (4)$$

Therefore, the (risk-free) interest rate is given by the stochastic Ramsey formula:

$$r^f = \rho + \eta\mu - \frac{1}{2}\eta^2\sigma^2 \tag{5}$$

Thus, uncertainty will always bring the risk-free rate down compared with the interest rate under the deterministic Ramsey formula because of the negative term, $-\frac{1}{2}\eta^2 \sigma^2$. The higher the uncertainty (measured as a higher σ), the more the risk-free interest rate comes down. But, with uncertainty, riskier assets have interest rates that differ from the risk-free interest rate. For example, the remuneration of equity (riskier) assets is:

$$r^f = \rho + \eta\mu - \frac{1}{2}\eta^2\sigma^2 + \eta\sigma^2 \tag{6}$$

Therefore, equity holders require an additional remuneration for holding risky assets, captured by the term $\eta\sigma^2$, which is a measure of the equity risk premium. In comparison with the deterministic Ramsey formula, re-writing the equity interest rate as:

$$r^e = \rho + \eta\mu + \eta\left(1\frac{\eta}{2}\right)\sigma^2 \tag{7}$$

Equation (7) shows that for values of ç lower than 2, the equity interest rate will always be higher than the deterministic Ramsey interest rate. In a more general framework, the rate of return on a composite asset $e^{-rt}$ may be calculated as the sum of the risk-free rate of return $e^{-rft}$ and a risk premium, $\beta(e^{ret}-e^{-rft})$, that t depends on β, which stands for the "quantity of risk" in the capital asset pricing models, measuring the correlation between the returns to the asset and the equity market returns.

$$e^{-rt} = e^{-rft} + \beta(e^{-ret} - e^{-rft}) \tag{8}$$

Thus, the interest rates used to discount an investment in assets with risk "in-between" the risk free rate and the (risky) equity rate are a (log) weighted average of the risk-free and risky interest rates:

$$r(t) = -\frac{\log\left|\beta e^{-ret} + (1-\beta)e^{-rft}\right|}{t} \tag{9}$$

If β is zero, then there is no risk so the discount rate becomes the risk-free rate $r^f$, and if β is one, then the asset is as risky as equity, so the discount rate becomes $r^e$.

In case of structural uncertainty unleashed by climate change, we are totally ignorant about the true values of the parameters in the distribution of growth rate g, the conventional "consumption smoothing" analysis developed using marginal reasoning no longer remains meaningful. One has to move towards justifications for catastrophe insurance to avoid extreme outcomes in the future. Chichilnisky (2000) introduced new decision criterion to represent how people rationalize the problem of making decisions in situations involving catastrophic risks. Such criteria are composed of two terms: one term that takes into account the maximization of expected utility and a second term that represents people's desire to avoid a catastrophe. Both parts are present, and both turn out to be important in making decisions under catastrophic risks. Weitzman (2007) developed a model of asset returns (also applicable to climate change) where people form their expectations based on a Bayesian estimation from a small sample and the best available estimate of the true probability distribution has fat tails.

Because people are assumed to be risk-averse, the attempt to avoid the small possibility of infinite losses dominates policy decisions. Weitzman, (2008), argues that it may be irrelevant to estimate the most likely level of climate damages; instead, what really counts is the worst-case scenario, i.e. how bad and how likely the worst extremes of the possible outcomes are. He summarizes the theorem as follows:

> *"in principle, what might be called the catastrophe-insurance aspect of such a fat-tailed unlimited-exposure situation, which can never be fully learned away, can dominate the social discounting aspect, the pure-risk aspect, and the consumption-smoothing aspect"*. (Weitzman, 2008).

The discussion on the determination of discounting so far has not considered the implications of asymmetries (heterogeneity) in preferences, the distribution of income, or other factors. The simpler models assume that the world could be represented by just one individual or a group of identical individuals at each point in time, consuming one goods or a basket of identical goods. But in reality, the world is not composed of a single individual or a group of identical individuals, and the impacts of climate change on different countries and communities will be very diverse. Thus, it is important to take inter-generational and intra-generational inequality into account and see how factoring in the asymmetries that exist in the world may affect the determination of global social discount rate. It is also worthwhile to note that the infinite horizon agent framework, pioneered by Ramsey, 1928, is only one way to analyze inter-temporal or inter-generational choice. One new direction in the economics of climate change is to use the overlapping generation (OLG) models, which assume a succession of generations to allow for easy modeling of agent heterogeneity. In each period, there are young agents (born this period) and elder agents (born last period). OLG models are thus intrinsically dynamic and can derive rich economic behaviour. As environmental policy questions often touch on inter-generational distribution, it is argued that OLG models may provide a superior framework than infinitely-lived representative agent models to characterize the behaviour of decision-makers. Howarth (1998) studied an OLG climate model and finds that the discount rate is contingent on policies that define the distribution of income between generations. Gerlagh and van der Zwaan (2001) used an OLG model to allow for a more flexible relationship between the discounting rate and economic growth.

Various factors can result in changes in the discount rate over time, such as local or global demographic changes (for example, the expected modification in life expectancy of local or global population), or a modification of the regime designed to prevent excess exploitations of the environment (for example, the possibility of establishing an environmental trust fund).

## SECTION III

## IMPLICATIONS FOR DEVELOPMENT POLICIES

The estimates of climate change induced catastrophies and the theoretical research on cost-benefit analysis of growth process under climate change induced long-term uncertainty and its mitigation, have important implications for the development process in general and in less developed countries in particular. The choice of a discount rate is critical because the flows to be discounted have a long time horizon in the case of climate change. One important variable policy-makers use to decide on mitigation strategies is the social cost of carbon (SCC) which is the value of the climate change impacts from 1 tonne of carbon emitted, aggregated over time and discounted back to the present day. It can be interpreted as the marginal global damage costs of carbon emissions. While the specific way in which discounting affects the outcomes of different climate policies is complex, in general, high social discount rates result in a lower SCC estimate and favour a "rampup" approach to mitigation, while low discount rates result in a higher SCC estimate and favour more immediate large-scale action. The results of Stern (2007) are all based on a single integrated assessment model, PAGE 2002 developed by Hope (2006a). However, Hope (2006b) also using PAGE 2002 but picking $\rho$ = 1-3%, $\eta$ = *1*, found that the mean SCC emitted in 2001 was only \$43 per tonne of carbon under both a business-as-usual scenario, and under a scenario aimed at stabilizing $CO_2$ concentrations at 550 ppm, which implied the SCC estimate was not sensitive to the path of emissions. Clearly, the SCC estimate was sensitive to a number of scientific and economic inputs to the model including the choice of the discount rate. When using $\rho$ = 0.1% in the same PAGE model. Hope (2006b) found that the SCC estimate went up from \$43 per tonne of carbon to \$365 per tonne of carbon.

A first policy implication of uncertainty may be that it is important to allow for flexibility in climate policy-making, including targets and strategies, whenever necessary and appropriate. Climate policies need to be sensitive and responsive to new information and progress made on further research on climate change science, economic modelling and policy analysis. As IPCC (2007) puts it, the challenge for policy-makers is not to find the best climate policy today for the next 100 years, but to select a prudent strategy and to adjust it over time in the light of new information. The implication is that in practice, when designing and implementing climate policies, it may be wise to keep many options open from both the analytical the policy perspective. A second policy implication is to emphasize the robustness and sensitivity check in climate policy modeling analysis. In practice, it may be worthwhile to check alternative scenarios and alternative climate change models. Instead of using a single discount rate, different discount rates can be applied depending on the period of time and the path. Third, public policy can play an important role in dealing with climate uncertainty in terms of promoting research on and awareness of climate change. Uncertainty implies opportunities for learning. Governments are probably best positioned to educate people about the urgency to stabilize the climate and to promote research on climate change science and economics through research grants and endowments. Especially, technological progress to reduce the cost of mitigation (for example, technologies to sequester carbon or reduce incoming solar radiation) could be explored and made possible with the support of public funding. Lastly, besides direct policy measures to cut emissions, it is also important for policy-makers to devote efforts to adaptation. As both adaptation and mitigation efforts are continuously reevaluated in the light of new information and findings, adopting a composite policy involving both adaptation and mitigation may be more effective. Creating an environment in which economic development can take place is seemed as another form of insurance since it will enable people who are currently vulnerable to the climate change to diversify their economic activities and thereby become more robust and sustainable in the face of climate challenges.

In the case of potentially catastrophic but highly uncertain climate change, the policy implication is quite clear. Given the structural uncertainties, the conventional "consumption smoothing" analysis developed using marginal reasoning is no longer meaningful. The combination of unknown structural uncertainty (probability distribution) and potentially catastrophic outcomes provides a motivation for precautionary policy in climate change, which implies making resource allocations today to "thin" the tails of the distribution of consumption growth rate to avoid extreme outcomes in the future. This catastrophe insurance argument is the same logic as the one motivating individuals to purchase earthquake or flood insurance. Thus, in spite of the concern that immediate and deep carbon emissions may slow the economy down, catastrophe insurance arguments provide an alternative framework (similar to using a very low discount rate in measuring the benefits of climate change mitigation policies) for policy-makers to take immediate actions today to avoid a potentially much larger, albeit uncertain, loss of income from some future catastrophic climate event. The greater are uncertainties, the greater is the risk of waiting.

There are important asymmetries that policy-makers need to keep in mind when making and implementing climate policies. On the one hand, asymmetries in contributions to the current stocks of greenhouse gases argue for the principle of "common but differentiated responsibility" to tackle climate change. On the other hand, climate change affects different regions and different groups of people differently (except for catastrophic climate events that are likely to leave every country and virtually every person worse-off). Near-term climate warming may be welcomed and valued positively in cold rich countries, while the climate effects in tropical regions are and will be overwhelmingly negative. There exist asymmetric views of posterity, valuation of environmental goods and aversion to losses among individuals linked with income distribution. Thus, the urge to act, the weight given to the future, the tolerance for risk, and other factors that determine how strongly and quickly we want to start addressing climate change will probably vary depending on people's place of residence and income level.

The asymmetries involved reveal that comparing costs and benefits across time or space using a single discount rate should be considered carefully. The conventional climate change policy-making based on a single constant global discount rate ignores important asymmetries in preferences, distribution of income, regional economic growth prospects and exhaustibility of consumption goods. These asymmetries suggest to policy-makers a lower discount rate, a higher estimate of SCC and make climate policies more likely to pass a cost benefit analysis. Various intra-generational asymmetries argue for a lower discount rate because climate change will have a disproportionate negative impact on the poor. If policy-makers are concerned about intra-generational inequality, a lower discount rate should be used also to avoid enlarging income disparities. A higher aversion to intra-temporal inequality will lower the discount rate.

Policy-makers concerned about inter-generational inequality probably would apply a lower "ethical" rate of pure time preference in climate risk assessments to evaluate benefits received by future generations, so as to not trivialize these benefits relative to current costs. In another case, if the consumption growth rate per capita actually would fall over time with the threat of climate change, it could lead to a lower discount rate. Especially if we project global consumption growth rates using population weights instead of GDP weights, the future negative effects of global warming on the growth of fast-growing populous developing economies will reduce the overall global growth rate even more compared to the GDP-weighted methodology. This could lead to an even lower discount rate and a stronger policy implication for immediate actions on climate change. The OLG framework provides policy-makers an alternative angle to account for the intergenerational asymmetry in their policy-making. The possibility of a more flexible relationship between the discount rate and economic growth implies various factors that may affect economic growth could also lead to a time-variant discount rate (often declining over time). Thus, incorporating those factors (local or global demographic changes or any environmental policy modifications) to climate policy-making will capture the inter-generational asymmetry. Climate policy-makers should also take into account the difference between environmental goods and other consumptions goods when evaluating different policy options. Re-pricing the future damages using the rising relative price of environmental goods could counteract the discounting effect and amplify climate damage estimates, which will thus suggest a much more urgent need for mitigation and adaptation. But mitigation and adaptation are costly, and for poor developing countries, such strategies require funding, other than those internally procured sources.

The task of initiating such mitigation exercises where the pollution and climate change are spilled over from advanced nations, becomes an issue of global cooperation and transfer of resources, which has ticklish political economy implications. Poor developing countries are particularly vulnerable to the adverse impacts of climate change because many of these economies depend on sectors that are susceptible to climate fluctuations, such as agriculture, fisheries, forestry and tourism. The economic development in some poor Asian and African countries is also threatened by increasingly severe water scarcity which is associated with the retreat of glaciers. Deteriorating water scarcity may lead to increasing competition between different sectors, different communities and different countries. Increasingly unpredictable weather patterns could result in reductions in crop yields which will push food prices higher and fuel social tensions. Sea level rise, increased natural disasters and the shrinking viable agricultural land may cause large-scale and destabilizing forced migration. The losses of income that are predicted if mitigation is taken up will fall on some countries and people more than others. For example, strong mitigation measures may hurt economies that are heavily dependent on fossil fuels. Within countries, many people that work in or are dependent on emission-intensive activities may be economically displaced. On the other hand, others argue that if no strong and immediate mitigations are taken, not only the whole world may be subject to catastrophic climate risks but also development progress made by poor countries can be completely erased by climate disasters.

Poorer countries are also less capable of adapting to the adverse impacts of climate change. The poorest countries and people are suffering the most in terms of the effects of climate change, and this pattern is likely to persist in the future. If this pattern does persist, climate change will hurt economic growth, drive income divergence and deepen global inequalities. The exposure of the poor to extreme weather risks is heavily skewed towards developing countries. As the financial needs to address climate change are large, global, and urgent, fairness and capacity concerns would argue that these financing needs should be met primarily by developed countries. It is unlikely that the developed countries would share the financial burden of mitigating costs with the developing nations, such that the prospects of economic growth in developing nations without risk of pollution and climate adversities would be constrained by their own ability to raise resources for mitigating such spilled over pollution and climate change, affecting its agriculture, river flows and livelihood uncertainties associated with such damages. For a country like India, the issue of financing mitigation costs to climate change would be enormous and given the fragility of its ongoing growth process under the neo-liberal regimes, it is expected that such exercises would not be undertaken effectively.

Climate change vagaries would affect the developing world in the following ways. First of all, weather variations and climatic catastrophes would affect the flow of water and would adversely affect the agricultural growth in developing countries, and thus food security, raising food prices and exposing the poor to inflationary shocks and hence more vulnerable. Secondly, the uncertainties caused by change in climatic conditions including disasters would warrant policy makers to choose between faster and more inclusive growth, thus affecting the income redistribution policies more ineffective in such countries, and compromising the social sector expenditures to mitigate the age-old deprivations in health and education and the incidence of poverty. Thirdly, it is important to take into account the impact of climate change on income distributions. Income distributions intersect with climate change at two levels: first, in terms of the causes of climate change (emissions of greenhouse gases) and second, in terms of the effects of climate change. In terms of causes of climate change, one should note the asymmetries across countries in the accumulation of global income over time. Although there is no direct correspondence between rich countries today and historical heavy emitters, partly because some heavily industrialized countries had fallen back economically, but there is no denying the fact today's richest countries have the overwhelming responsibility for the accumulated stocks of greenhouse gases in the atmosphere. If we look at today's emissions—that is, flows rather than stocks—rich countries remain important emitters, but a few large erstwhile developing countries have also started to contribute significantly. Within a country also, particularly in the developing countries, there are sharp inequalities in income and assets across regions and persons and climate change is likely to affect the most poor and vulnerable sections of population in such countries compared to others who are relatively better placed in the income distribution ladder. Effective protection to these vulnerable groups against climatic disorders and disasters are important challenges faced by the developing nations.

For a country like India, which is home to a large section of world's vulnerable section of population (about a third), mostly habited in rural areas and are directly dependent on climate-sensitive resources such as agriculture, forests and river water, the effect of climate change induced calamities are likely to be severe. The agricultural sector of its economy is likely to be severely affected by the change in climate, rising heat, rising sea levels or river depletion, and it is estimated that with every one degree Celsius rise in global temperature, India would lose four to five million tonnes in wheat production, thus raising food prices and harming food security of the masses. Add to this are the costs of disasters induced by climate variations, displacements, disease and infrastructural damages, and the challenge seems even grimmer. All these are likely to result in resource-based conflicts which would amplify the social and political tensions that would constrain the growth process of the economy. Secondly, with increasing trends of urbanization in India, the emission levels are likely to grow and the pitfalls of environmental hazards following such emissions are likely to fall more on the poor and the vulnerable than the higher echelons of her income distribution.

## SECTION IV

## CONCLUSIONS

The phenomenon of climate change and the disasters induced by it pose important challenge to the development programmes of nations. The changes that are occurring at the global level have important spill-over effects, and given the asymmetry of the impacts and the asymmetry of the distribution of income and wealth across countries and populations, the threats to livelihoods and to long-term sustainability of the growth process in the developing countries, the initiatives are likely to be divergent and yet the tasks are quite large in nature For the developing countries like India, mitigation for climate change induced disasters would warrant transfer of funds from the advanced countries and international cooperation in this area is required to finance such mitigation costs. The task of policy planners in developing countries is to chart out development strategy that would keep the tempo of growth unchecked, yet the benefits need to be trickled down to the vulnerable sections of its populations so that they could minimize the risk of such disasters as may be due to change in global temperature and emissions. The threat to long-term sustainability of the growth process of the developing countries trying to catch-up with the advanced nations of today is serious and so also the threat to livelihood security of the vast majority of poor and vulnerable sections of the population who are concentrated in the developing countries of Asia, Africa and Latin America. Climate change poses serious challenge to the design and implementation of development programmes in these poor countries.

### REFERENCES

ADB (2009), "The Economics of Climate Change in Southeast Asia: a Regional Review." Jakarta: Asian Development Bank.

Arrow, Kenneth J. (1995), 'Intergenerational Equality and the Rate of Discount in Long-term Social Investment', IEA World Congress Paper, Stanford University.

Batissi and Naylor, Battisti, David and Rosamond Naylor (2009), "Historical Warnings of Future Food Insecurity with Unprecedented Seasonal Heat." *Science,* 323: 240-244.

Brown, Oli and Alec Crawford. (2009),"Climate Change and Security in Africa." Working Paper. IISD (International Institute for Sustainable Development), Winnipeg, Canada.

Brown, Peter (1998), 'Tow d an Economics of Stewardship: the Case of Climate', *Ecological Economics* 26, 11-21.

Böhner, Jürgen and Frank Lehmkuhl (2005), "Environmental Change Modeling for Central and High Asia: Pleistocene, Present and Future Scenarios." *Boreas,* 34: 220-31.

Chichilnisky Graciela (2000), 'An Axiomatic Approach to Choice under Uncertainty with Catastrophic Risks', *Resource and Energy Economics,* 22: 221-31.

Church, J.A. *et al.* (2009), "Changes in global upper-ocean heat content over the last half century and comparison with climate models", IOP Conference Series: Earth and Environmental Sciences.

Cline, William. (2007), *Global Warming and Agriculture: Impact Estimates by Country.* Washington, DC: Peterson Institute for International Economics.

Conceição, Pedro and Zhang, Yanchun (2009), Discounting in the Context of Climate Change Economics: The Policy Implications of Uncertainty and Global Asymmetries, A UNDP/ODS Working Paper Office of Development Studies United Nations Development Programme, New York, March 2009.

Dasgupta, Partha (2007), Commentary: the Stern Review's on Economics of Climate Change. National Institute Economic Review, 2007, 199, pp. 4-7.

Dell, Melissa, Benjamin Jones, and Benjamin Olken (2009), "Temperature and Income: Reconciling New Cross-Sectional and Panel Estimates." *American Economic Review: Papers and Proceedings,* 99: 198-204.

Domingues, Catia *et al.* 2008. "Improved estimates of upper-ocean warming and multi-decadal sea-level rise." *Nature,* 453: 1090-94.

Galeotti, Marzio, Alessandro Lanza and Francesco Pauli(2006), "Reassessing the Environmental Kuznets Curve for $CO_2$ Emissions: a Robustness Exercise." *Ecological Economics,* 57: 152-63.

Gerlagh, Reyer and B.C.C. van der Zwaan (2001), 'The Effects of Ageing and an Environmental Trust Fund in an Overlapping Generations Model on Carbon Emission Reductions', *Ecological Economics,* 36: 311-26.

Grinsted, Aslak *et al.* (2009), "Reconstructing Sea Level from Paleo and Projected Temperatures 200 to 2100 A.D." Climate Dynamics. [http://dx.doi.org/10.1007/s00382-008-0507-2].

Gollier, Christian and Richard Zeckhauser (2005), 'Aggregation of Heterogeneous Time Preferences', *Journal of Political Economy,* 113: 878-96.

Harrod, Roy (1948), *Towards a Dynamic Economics,* London: Macmillan.

Hope, Chris (2006a), 'The Marginal Impact of $CO_2$ from PAGE 2002: An Integrated Assessment Model Incorporating the IPCC's Five Reasons for Concern', *Integrated Assessment Journal,* 6: 19-56.

Hope, Chris (2006b), 'The social cost of carbon: What does it actually depend on?', *Climate Policy,* 6: 566–77.

Howarth, Richard (1998), 'An Overlapping Generations Model of Climate-Economy Interactions', *Scandinavian Journal of Economics,* 100: 575-91.

———, (2007), 'Towards an Operational Sustainability Criterion', *Ecological Economics,* 63:656-663.

———, (2009), 'Discounting, Uncertainty, and Revealed Time Preference', *Land Economics,* 85: 24-40.

IFPRI (2009), "Climate Change Impact on Agriculture and Cost of Adaptation". Food Policy Report. Washington D.C.: International Food Policy Research Institute.

IMF (International Monetary Fund). 2003. "Fund Assistance for Countries Facing Exogenous Shocks." Policy Development and Review Departments, Washington DC.

Innovas (2009), "Low Carbon and Environmental Goods and Services: an Industry Analysis." Commissioned Report for UK Department for Business Enterprise & Regulatory Reform: London.

IIPCC (Inter-governmental Panel on Climate Change). (2007), *Climate Change 2007: The Physical Science Basis. Contribution of Working Group I to the Fourth Assessment Report of the Inter-governmental Panel on Climate Change.* Cambridge: Cambridge University Press.

Koopmans, Tjalling C. (1965), 'On the Concept of Optimal Economic Growth', In *The Economic Approach to Development Planning,* Amsterdam: Elsevier.

Levina, Ellina (2007), *Adaptation to Climate change: International agreements for local needs.*Paris: Organisation for Economic Co-operation and Development.

McKinsey (2009), "Pathways to a Low-Carbon Economy: Version 2 of the Global Greenhouse Gas Abatement Cost Curve." McKinsey & Company.

Nellemann, C., MacDevette, M., Manders, T., Eickhout, B., Svihus, B., Prins, A.G., Kaltenborn, B.P. (Eds.). 2009. *The Environmental Food Crisis—The environment's role in averting future food crises—A UNEP rapid response assessment.* United Nations Environment Programme. Norway: GRID-Arendal.

Nordhaus, William D. (1994), *Managing the Global Commons: The Economics of Climate Change,* Cambridge, Massachusetts: MIT Press.

———, (2007), 'A Review of the Stern Review on the Economics of Global Warming', *Journal of Economic Literature,* 45: 686-702.

Oxfam (2007), "Adapting to Climate Change: What's Needed in Poor Countries and Who Should Pay". http://www.oxfam.org/en/files/bp104_climate_change_0705.pdf/download].

Padukone Neil (2010), Climate Change in India: Forgotten Threats, Forgotton Opportunities, *Economic and Political Weekly,* Vol XLV, No. 22, May 29, 2010.

Pigou, A.C. (1932), *The Economics of Welfare,* 4th edition, London: Macmillan.

Pfeffer, Tad *et al.* (2008), "Kinematic Constraints on Glacier Contributions to 21st-Century Sea-Level Rise." *Science* 321: 1340-43.

Quiggin, John (2008), 'Uncertainty and Climate Change Policy', *Economic Analysis & Policy,* 38: 203-10.

Ramsey, Frank P. (1928), 'A Mathematical Theory of Saving', *Economic Journal,* 38 (December): 543-59.

Renner, Michael, Sean Sweeney and Jill Kubit (2008), "Green Jobs: Towards a Decent Work in a Sustainable, Low-Carbon World." UNEP/ILO/IOE/ITUC, Geneva.

Richardson, Katherine *et al.* (2009). "Synthesis Report." Report prepared for Climate Change: Global Risks, Challenges & Decisions Conference, 10-12 March, Copenhagen.

Robinson, John, *et al.* 2006. "Climate Change and Sustainable Development: Realizing the opportunity." *Ambio* 35: 2-8.

Sokolov, Andrei *et al.* (2009), "Probabilistic forecast for 21st century climate based on uncertainties in emissions (without policy) and climate parameters." Report 169. MIT Joint Program on the Science and Policy of Global Change, Cambridge, Mass.

Solow, Robert (1974), 'The Economics of Resources or the Resources of Economics', *American Economic Review,* 64:1-14.

Stern, David (2004), "The Rise and Fall of the Environmental Kuznets Curve." *World Development,* 32: 1419-39.

Stern, Nick *et al.* (2009), "Low-Carbon Growth: The Only Sustainable Way to Overcome World Poverty." Development in a Changing Climate Blog. World Bank: Washington D.C.

Stern, Nicholas *et al.* (2007), *The Economics of Climate Change,* Cambridge, UK: Cambridge University Press.

Tol, Richard and Gary Yohe (2006), 'A Review of the Stern Review,' *World Economics,* 7: 233-50.

Thompson, Lonnie *et al.* (2002), "Kilimanjaro Ice Core Records: Evidence of Holocene Climate Change in Tropical Africa." *Science,* 298: 589-93.

UNDP (2007),. *Human Development Report, 2007/2008: Fighting Climate Change: Human Solidarity in a Divided World.* New York: United Nations Development Programme.

UNFCCC (2008). "Investment and Financial Flows to Address Climate Change: an Update". FCCC/TP/2008/7. Poznan, November, 2008.

Weitzman, Martin L. (1998), 'Why the Far-Distant Future Should be Discounted at Its Lowest Possible Rate', *Journal of Environmental Economics and Management,* 36: 201-08.

Weitzman, Martin (2007), The Stern Review of the Economics of Climate Change. *Journal of Economic Literature,* 45(3), pp. 703-24 (2007).

Weitzman, Martin L. (2009), On Modeling and Interpreting the Economics of Catastrophic Climate Change. *Review of Economics and Statistics,* February 2009.

Weitzman, Martin L. (2009), Some Basic Economics of Extreme Climate Change, Working Paper, Harvard University, February 19, 2009.

World Bank (2006), World Bank. 2006. Clean Energy and Development: Towards an Investment Framework, Washington, D.C: World Bank.

Zhang, Yanchun (2009), Climate Change and Development: Interlinked Challenges and Opportunities, A UNDP/ODS Working Paper, Office of Development Studies, United Nations Development Programme, New York, December 2009.

# 2

# Trade and Climate Change

Over the last few years, climate change has moved to the forefront of public attention, media headlines and political discourse. It has become increasingly clear that climate change is one of the greatest challenges the world has ever faced. The scientific evidence regarding climate change is compelling. It is estimated that, over the last century, the global average surface temperature has increased by about 0.74°C. Moreover, many greenhouse gases remain in the atmosphere for long periods of time, and as a result global warming will continue to affect the natural systems of the planet for several hundred years, even if emissions were reduced substantially or halted today. Current estimates of climate change have calculated that global average temperatures will increase by 1.4° to 6.4°C between 1990 and 2100. As greenhouse gas emissions and temperatures increase, the impacts from climate change are expected to become more widespread and to intensify A global consensus is emerging that the increase in atmospheric temperature should be limited to around 2°C above pre- industrial levels in order to prevent the worst impacts of climate changes. In order to keep temperatures within this range, the IPCC's Fourth Assessment Report argues that global greenhouse gas (GHG) emissions must start declining by 2015. For industrialized countries, which are responsible for most of the GHGs already in the atmosphere, this implies implementing drastic cuts immediately; the latest IPCC Report suggests that compared to 1990 levels, industrialized countries might have to reduce their emissions by 25 to 40 per cent by 2020 and 80 to 95 per cent by 2050. The distribution of these weather events, however, is expected to vary considerably among regions and countries, and impacts will depend to a large extent on the vulnerability of populations or ecosystems. Developing countries, and particularly the poorest and most marginalized populations within these countries, will generally be both the most adversely affected by the impacts of future climate change and the most vulnerable to its effects, because they are less able to adapt than developed countries and populations. In addition, climate change risks compound the other challenges which are already faced by these countries, including tackling poverty, improving health care, increasing food security and improving access to sources of energy. Although the impacts of climate change are specific to location and to the level of development, most sectors of the global economy are expected to be affected and these impacts will often have implications for trade. Three trade-related areas are considered to be particularly vulnerable to climate change: *Agriculture, Tourism, and trade infrastructure and routes*.

The structure of the present essay is as follows. Section I outlines the link between international trade and climate change. This is followed by a discussion on the assessments of the effect of trade opening on emissions in section II. Section III discusses the effects of international trade on impacts of greenhouse gas emissions due to the transport sector activities, while section IV outlines trade and environment negotiations under the WTO and section V discusses the contribution of trade and trade opening to climate change mitigation and adaptation efforts. Section VI summarises the main conclusions of the paper.

## Section I

## INTERNATIONAL TRADE AND CLIMATE CHANGE

The past half a century has experienced an unprecedented expansion of international trade. In terms of volume, world trade is nearly thirty-two times greater than it was in 1950, and the share of global GDP it represents rose from 5.5 per cent in 1950 to 21 per cent in 2007. During this sixty-year period, trade expanded at an even faster pace than it did during the first wave of globalization in the late 19th to early 20th centuries. This dramatic expansion may be one reason why trade is increasingly being taken into consideration in climate change discussions. A number of reasons have been given to explain the enormous expansion in world trade. Foremost among these reasons is technological change, which has dramatically reduced the cost of transportation and communications. In the second half of the 20th century, the introduction of the jet engine and the use of containers in the transportation of goods (allowing rapid and efficient loading, unloading and transfer of shipments) have significantly reduced the cost of air and maritime transportation (Hummels, 2007). This, in turn, expanded the range and volume of goods that could be traded. The information and communication technology (ICT) revolution led to a dramatic reduction in the cost of communications, making it easier, for example, to coordinate the production of a final good whose parts and components may have been produced in several different countries (referred to as "unbundling" production). A second reason for the expansion in trade is the spread of more open trade and investment policies. Many countries have liberalized their trade regimes through unilateral changes in their national policies, through bilateral or regional trade arrangements, or through multilateral trade negotiations. Thus, technological innovations and the opening of trade and investment policies have both increased participation in trade and, at the same time, made it easier to "unbundle" production across a range of countries. The parts and components that make up a final product may be manufactured in different locations around the globe. Many of these manufacturing plants are located in developing countries that, as a result, become increasingly integrated in global supply chains.

This phenomenal expansion in global trade has raised questions such as: "Will trade opening lead to more greenhouse gas emissions? "and "How much does trade change greenhouse gas emissions?" Trade opening can affect the amount of emissions in three principal ways, which are typically referred to as the scale, composition and technique effects. The *scale effect* refers to the expansion of economic activity arising from trade opening, and its effect on greenhouse gas emissions. This increased level of economic activity will require greater energy use and will therefore lead to higher levels of greenhouse gas emissions. The *composition effect* describes the way that trade opening changes the structure of a country's production in response to changes in relative prices, and the consequences of this on emission levels. The effect on a country's greenhouse gas emissions will depend on whether a country has a comparative advantage in emission-intensive sectors and whether these sectors are expanding or contracting. The composition of production in an economy that is opening its markets to trade may also be a response to differences in environmental regulations between countries (resulting in the "pollution haven hypothesis", which suggests that high-emission industries may relocate to countries with less stringent emission regulation policies). Finally, the *technique effect* refers to improvements in the methods by which goods and services are produced, so that the emission intensity of output is reduced. This is the principal way in which trade opening can help mitigate climate change.

A decline in greenhouse gas emission intensity can come about in two ways. First, more open trade can increase the availability, and lower the cost of, climate-friendly goods and services. This will help meet the demand in countries whose domestic industries do not produce these climate-friendly goods and services in sufficient quantities or at affordable prices. Second, as income levels rise because of trade opening, populations may demand lower greenhouse gas emissions. For rising income to lead to environmental improvement, governments must supply the appropriate tax and regulatory measures to meet the public's demand. Since greenhouse gas emissions are released into the atmosphere, and since part of the cost is borne by populations in other countries, there may not be a strong incentive for any given nation to take action to reduce such emissions, even if its citizens' incomes are improving. Since the scale and technique effects tend to work in opposite directions, and the composition effect depends on the comparative advantage of countries and on differences in regulations between countries, the overall impact of trade on greenhouse gas emissions cannot be determined *a priori*. The net impact of greenhouse gas emissions will depend on the magnitude or strength of each of the three effects, and ascertaining this requires detailed empirical analyses.

Climate change has significant impacts on all of society, including the economy. It is estimated that the impacts of unabated climate change would be equivalent to a loss of at least 5 per cent of global gross domestic product (GDP) each year and could reach as much as 20 per cent of global GDP. Climate change presents particular risks for developing countries. For instance, even if average temperatures were stabilized at 2.5°C above pre-industrial levels, 75–250 million people in Africa would experience water stress as early as 2020 as a consequence. Some countries in Africa may also suffer from a 50 per cent decline in agricultural yields. In general, the IPCC found a profound risk to the productive base in agriculture, forestry and fisheries in many developing countries. These are precisely the economic sectors that many of these countries depend on for export revenue. If the world is to avoid the worst impacts of climate change a fundamental restructuring of the economy is needed that places it onto a low-carbon path. Climate Change also brings huge economic opportunities. According to one measure from the Stern Review, the benefits over time of actions to shift the world onto a low-carbon path could be in the order of US$ 2.5 trillion each year and markets for low-carbon technologies would be worth at least US$ 500 billion, and perhaps much more by 2050 if the world acts on the scale required. The required change in consumption and production patterns will neither be easy to achieve nor occur without seriously altering global trade patterns. In addition, approaches to reduce GHG emissions might affect the international competitiveness of countries and hence reduce their willingness to endorse or implement such measures. Both climate change and measures taken to combat it will thus have an impact on international trade. Conversely, trade also impacts on climate change, in both synergistic and detrimental ways. For instance, it can spur the proliferation of climate-friendly technologies, yet it also stimulates economic activities that induce increased GHG emissions and leads to increased transportation of goods.

International Trade involves a process of exchange requiring that goods be transported from the place of production to the place of consumption. Consequently, international trade expansion is likely to lead to increased use of transportation services. Merchandise trade can be transported by air, road, rail and water. Maritime transport accounts for the bulk of international trade by volume and for a significant share by value. Recent studies indicate that, excluding trade within the European

Union, seaborne cargo accounted for 89.6 per cent of world trade by volume and 70.1 per cent of global trade by value in 2006. International maritime shipping, however, accounted for only 11.8 per cent of the transport sector's total contribution to $CO_2$ emissions. Aviation represents an 11.2 per cent share of $CO_2$ emissions, rail transport constitutes another 2 per cent share and road transport has the biggest share, at 72.6 per cent of the total $CO_2$ emissions from transport. Among the different modes of transport, shipping is the most carbon emission efficient, and this should be taken into account when assessing the contribution of trade to transport-related emissions.

Secondly, international trade can serve as a channel for spreading technologies that mitigate climate change. The spread of technological knowledge made possible by trade provides one mechanism by which developing countries can benefit from developed countries' innovations in climate change technology. There are several ways in which this transmission of technology can occur. One is through the import of intermediate and capital goods which a country could not have produced on its own. Second, trade may increase communication opportunities between countries, allowing developing countries to learn about production methods and design from developed countries. Third, international trade can increase the available opportunities for adapting foreign technologies to meet local conditions. Finally, the learning process made possible by international economic relations reduces the cost of future innovation and imitation. Beyond offering opportunities for mitigation, trade can also play a valuable role in helping humankind adapt to a warmer future. Climate change threatens to alter geographical patterns of production, with food and agricultural products likely to be the most affected. Trade can provide a means to bridge differences in demand and supply, so that countries where climate change creates scarcity are able to meet their needs by importing from countries where these goods and services continue to be available.

Trade economists have developed a conceptual framework to examine how trade opening may affect the environment. This framework, first used to study the environmental impact of the North American Free Trade Agreement (NAFTA), breaks down the impact of trade opening into three "effects": the scale effect (i.e. how greenhouse gas emissions may increase as a result of increased economic activity); the composition effect (i.e. the way trade opening, and consequent changes in relative prices, may affect the relative size of the various sectors that make up a country's production); and the technique effect (i.e. the manner in which technological improvements may be adopted to reduce the emission-intensity of the production of goods and services) (Grossman and Krueger, 1993).

Copeland and Taylor (2003) provide a definition of these effects from a general equilibrium model of trade and the environment. Some international organizations, such as the Organization for Economic

Cooperation and Development (OECD) (1994), have adopted or extended this conceptual framework in order to evaluate the environmental impact of trade agreements. This analytic framework can be applied to investigate the link between trade and climate change. While the scale effect may worsen climate change, the technique effect may help to mitigate it. There is some uncertainty, however, about the impact the composition effect would have on climate change. The "scale effect" refers to the increase in greenhouse gas emissions resulting from an expanded level of economic activity. According to Copeland and Taylor (2004), the scale effect can be defined as the increase in the value of production, measured in world prices as they were prior to trade opening. If there are unemployed resources (labour, capital or land) prior to liberalization, trade opening will allow greater utilization of these resources and will thus lead to an expansion in the level of production. This increased level of economic activity will, in turn, require greater energy use and since most countries rely on fossil fuels as their primary energy source, the scale effect will lead to higher levels of greenhouse gas emissions. Furthermore, increased trade will give rise to a greater use of cross-border transportation services, which will increase greenhouse gas emissions even further. The scale effect is conceptually different from economic growth, since the latter is a result of capital accumulation, population growth and technological change. Nevertheless, there is a presumption that, in theory, greater trade opening will lead to economic growth through (indirect) mechanisms that affect the rate of capital accumulation and improvements in productivity. Given that economic growth is closely linked with energy use, this will magnify the impact on greenhouse gas emissions. Despite this, it has not been easy to demonstrate a statistically significant relationship between trade barriers, in the form of tariff and non-tariff measures, and the rate of economic growth (Baldwin, 2000). In the 1990s, a number of studies appeared to show that "open" economies (with liberal trade policies) grew faster than "closed" economies. Dollar (1992), for example, estimated that the growth rate of Latin American and African economies would increase by between 1.5 and 2.1 per cent if they adopted more open trade policies. A study by Sachs and Warner (1995) finds that developing countries with more open trade policies grew at a rate of 4.5 per cent per year, while closed economies grew by only 0.7 per cent per year. However, these studies have been criticized for the use of measures of openness which are closely linked with other indicators of good economic performance, such as lack of restrictions on foreign exchange markets (Rodriguez and Rodrik, 1999). There is also a problem involving the endogeneity of trade and growth (Edwards, 1998). This refers to the possibility of a two-way rather than a one-way relationship between trade and economic growth. In other words, while more trade may have a positive impact on economic growth, growth may, in turn, lead to an increase in trade. Thus, a positive relationship between trade and growth does not automatically tell us that trade is causing higher growth. Baldwin's (2000) survey is careful to point out, however, that these problems should not be interpreted as indicating that international economic policies in general or international trade have only an insignificant effect on economic growth. The "composition effect" refers to the way that trade opening changes the share that each sector represents in a country's production in response to changes in relative prices, resulting in the expansion of some sectors and the contraction of others. The consequent increase or decrease of greenhouse gas emissions will depend on whether the emission-intensive sectors are expanding or contracting. Changes in the structure of a liberalizing country's production will depend on where the country's "comparative advantage" (in terms of resources and capacity) lies: if its comparative advantage is in sectors which are less emission-intensive, then trade opening will lead to lower greenhouse gas emissions, but if it is in the more emission-intensive sectors, then liberalization will lead to greater emissions of greenhouse gas. In addition, the "pollution-haven hypothesis" implies that the composition of production in a liberalizing economy will also respond to differences between countries in environmental regulations. If a country has stringent environmental protection measures in place, the increased competition brought about by trade opening may lead emission-intensive sectors to relocate to countries with weaker regulations. In the context of greenhouse gas emissions, the effect of international differences in climate change policies raises the likelihood of "carbon leakage". This term refers to a situation in which the measures taken by some countries to limit their carbon dioxide ($CO_2$) emissions at a national level do not ultimately result in a global $CO_2$ reduction, because industries emitting high levels of $CO_2$ simply relocate to countries which do not impose such strong penalties on emissions. Changes in the composition of the liberalizing country's production, whether resulting from its "comparative advantage" or from the pollution-haven hypothesis, will have an effect on how the production of its trade partners is changed. If trade opening results in a country producing fewer emission-intensive goods, then they must be procured elsewhere, giving rise to an expansion in the production of those goods in other parts of the world. The pattern of expansion and contraction of certain sectors of industry in the liberalizing country will be mirrored in reverse in the rest of the world. This suggests that trade opening can lead to some countries "specializing" in more emission-intensive industries, while other countries concentrate on "cleaner" industries. The net effect on greenhouse gas emissions at the global level will depend on the relative strengths of these effects. Finally, the technique effect refers to improvements in the methods by which goods and services are produced, so that the quantity of emissions released during the production process declines.

Following Grossman and Krueger (1993), this reduction in greenhouse gas emission may come about in two ways. First, more open trade will increase the availability and lower the cost of climate-friendly goods and services. This is particularly important for countries which do not have access to climate-friendly goods and services, or whose domestic industries do not produce such goods and services in sufficient amounts or at affordable prices. Access to the technologies used in the production of climate-friendly goods and services should reduce the energy required during production, and thus reduce emissions. For exporters, the prospect of increased market access would provide an incentive to develop new goods and services that help mitigate climate change. Such potential benefits of more open trade highlight the importance of the current negotiations under the Doha Round, which aim to liberalize environmental goods and services. Second, the increase in income levels that trade opening brings about can lead the general public to demand lower greenhouse gas emissions (a cleaner environment is a "normal" good). Increased incomes or wealth gives populations the freedom to be concerned about other aspects of their well-being, such as better environmental quality. Grossman and Krueger (1993) conjecture that this public demand is perhaps the most important outcome of the technique effect. For rising income to lead to environmental improvement, however, governments need to respond to the public's demands with the appropriate fiscal and regulatory measures. Only if such measures are put in place will firms adopt cleaner production technologies, so that a given level of output can be produced with lower greenhouse gas emissions than previously. Torras and Boyce (1998), who examined the available evidence on international variations in seven indicators of air and water quality, find that the degree of inequality in incomes, as well as inequalities in levels of literacy, political rights and civil liberties, had a substantial impact on the quality of environmental protection in low-income countries. Countries which had a more equitable distribution of income and which achieved greater equality in literacy, political rights and civil liberties tended to have better environmental quality. This evidence suggests that increases in income from trade opening may not translate into environmental improvements if the economic benefits are not shared more equitably among the population. While trade openness does not appear to be a major factor in income inequality in developed countries, the evidence is more mixed for developing countries. Due to the opposing nature of the scale and technique effects, Grossman and Krueger's study suggests that the relationship between per capita income and environmental quality may be non-linear. For countries with low levels of per capita income, increased economic growth may initially lead to deterioration of environmental quality. Only once a certain income threshold has been crossed do further increases in per capita income lead to gains in environmental quality.

## SECTION II

## ASSESSMENTS OF THE EFFECT OF TRADE OPENING ON EMISSIONS

We now focus on the available evidence about the effects of trade and trade opening on greenhouse gas emissions. Much of this literature is recent, and the body of work continues to grow. Most of the econometric studies suggest that more open trade would be likely to increase $CO_2$ emissions. It would appear that the scale effect tends to dominate the technique and composition effects. Some studies, however, suggest that there may be differences in impact on emissions between developed and developing countries, with improvement being observed in OECD countries and deterioration in developing countries. Although many developed countries now require environmental assessments of any trade agreements that they enter into, these assessments tend to focus on national rather than cross-border or global pollutants. A few of these assessments have raised concerns about the possible increase in greenhouse gas emissions from increased transport activity, although few have attempted a detailed quantitative analysis of the effects on emission levels of increased transportation.

### (a) Econometric Studies on the Scale, Composition and Technique Effects

Since the pioneering study by Grossman and Krueger on the impact of NAFTA on emissions of sulphur dioxide, more and more econometric studies have examined the environmental impact of trade openness. A study by Antweiller, Copeland and Taylor (2001), which estimates the scale, composition and technique effects using a general equilibrium model of trade and environment, also looks at sulphur dioxide emissions. A more recent study by Grether, Mathys and de Melo (2007) analyzes the impact of trade on worldwide sulphur dioxide emissions. For the most part, these studies tend to find that the technique effect played the dominant role: in all three studies, the technique effect was strong enough that trade opening resulted in environmental improvements. None of these studies, however, has examined greenhouse gas emissions, although this situation has started to change with the growing awareness of the problems posed by climate change. In econometric studies, it is often more convenient to analyze a cross-section of countries than to study the effects over time within a single country, since there are more observations available for analysis. This means, however, that countries may be observed at a point when no trade opening is taking place. One remedy to this problem is to use the degree of trade *openness*, which is usually defined as the proportion represented by trade (exports plus imports) in GDP, as a stand-in for the degree of trade *liberalization*. Of course, there may also be a separate interest in knowing how the trade orientation of a country (how open it is relative to other countries) affects its greenhouse gas emissions. Following the approach of Antweiller, Copeland and Taylor, a study by Cole and Elliott (2003a) considers the effect of trade openness on four environmental indicators, including carbon dioxide ($CO_2$) emissions. The data on $CO_2$ which they used covered 32 developed and developing countries during the period 1975-95. They find that, overall, more trade openness would be likely to increase $CO_2$ emissions, due to a large scale effect and only a small technique effect (in other words, increased trade openness would lead to increased production and therefore increased emissions, without a large enough increase in the use of emission-reduction technologies to counter such growth). For the median country in their sample, the composition effect was also positive, with a 1 per cent increase in trade intensity increasing per capita $CO_2$ emissions by 0.04 per cent. Frankel and Rose (2005) examine evidence from several countries on the relationship between seven indicators of environmental quality (including $CO_2$ emissions) and trade openness, for a given level of per capita income. In the case of $CO_2$ emissions, their data allows them to study nearly 150 countries. Their paper also takes account of the possible "endogeneity" of trade and per capita income through the use of instrumental variables techniques. The endogeneity of trade openness and per capita income arises because there may be a two-way rather than a one-way relationship between trade openness and per capita income. In other words, while more openness may increase per capita income, the latter may in turn lead to increased trade. When this endogeneity is not taken into account, the statistical results of their study indicate that trade openness would lead to increased $CO_2$ emissions. On the other hand, by including the possible endogeneity of trade in their calculations, the detrimental effect of trade openness on $CO_2$ emissions becomes statistically insignificant. Nevertheless, Frankel and Rose conclude that the main instance where trade and growth might have a detrimental effect is on the amount of $CO_2$ emissions. They recognize that this is due to the global nature of the externality (emissions are released into the global commons and the costs of the pollution are partly borne by foreigners) and that, as a result, $CO_2$ emissions are unlikely to be addressed by national environmental regulations. McCarney and Adamowicz (2005) use "panel data" for 143 countries, spanning the period 1976 to 2000, to examine the link between trade openness and $CO_2$ emissions. Their results indicate that more open trade significantly increases emissions of $CO_2$, although they are not able to give a breakdown of the overall outcome into the individual contributions of the scale, composition and technique effects. The fact that the data covered differences between countries over different periods of time allowed heterogeneity across countries to be taken into account, so that comparisons could be drawn about how different national characteristics influence the environmental impact of more open trade. One such difference among the countries that they examined is the effect of democratic governance, as compared to autocratic governance.

Interestingly, they find that greater democracy may be linked to increased levels of $CO_2$ emissions. In their view, this may be the result of an indirect effect of governance on environmental quality, whereby the lack of good governance reduces prosperity, thus reducing per capita income levels and, in consequence, emissions. Managi (2005) uses data for 63 developed and developing countries over the period 1960 to 1999 to examine the link between trade openness and levels of $CO_2$ emissions. As in the case of the study by Frankel and Rose, the possibility of endogeneity between trade openness and income was taken into account in the estimation. The results of the study suggest that further trade opening would result in increased emissions with an estimated elasticity (a measure of the responsiveness of $CO_2$ emissions to trade openness) of 0.579, with a greater contribution from the scale effect than from the technique effect. However, a later study by Managi *et al.* (2008) suggests that the impact of trade openness on $CO_2$ emissions may differ between developed countries (OECD members) and developing countries. They estimate the overall impact of trade openness on emission levels of carbon dioxide and sulphur dioxide, and on levels of biochemical oxygen demand (BOD)—a measure of the amount of oxygen used by micro-organisms while breaking down organic matter in water, which is used as an indicator of pollution levels. They use panel data on $CO_2$ and $CO_2$ emissions of 88 countries from 1973 to 2000 and the BOD levels of 83 countries from 1980to 2000. The econometric analysis they employed allows them to correct for the endogeneity of income and trade and enabled them to distinguish between the short-term and long-term relationships between trade and $CO_2$ emissions. They find that trade openness reduces $CO_2$ emissions in OECD countries because the technique effect dominates the scale and composition effects, but that it has a detrimental effect on carbon dioxide emissions in non-OECD countries, where the scale and composition effects prevail over the technique effect. They also find that the long-term impact of tradeon $CO_2$ emission levels is large, although it is small in the short-term.

## (b) The "Environmental Kuznets Curve" and Greenhouse Gas Emissions

A separate subsection looks at the empirical evidence on whether an environmental Kuznets curve exists for greenhouse gas emissions. This literature has produced inconsistent results, although recent studies tend to show that no such curve exists for $CO_2$ emissions. Studies that differentiate between OECD and non-OECD countries tend to find an environmental Kuznets curve for the first group of countries but not for the second. Three aspects of the empirical literature on trade opening and emission levels have been reviewed: econometric or statistical studies of the effects of trade opening on emissions; estimates of the "environmental Kuznets curve" for greenhouse gases (which describes the relationship between higher per capita incomes and lower greenhouse gas emissions); and assessments—carried out by the parties to various trade agreements of the environmental impact of these agreements. Most of the statistical studies reviewed indicate that more open trade will most likely lead to increased $CO_2$ emissions, and suggest that the scale effect tends to offset the technique and composition effects. Some studies indicate, however, that there may be differences in outcomes between developed and developing countries, with environmental improvement being observed in OECD countries and environmental deterioration in developing countries. The empirical literature on the environmental Kuznets curve for greenhouse gas emissions has produced inconsistent results, although the more recent studies tend to show that there is no relationship between higher income and lower $CO_2$ emissions. Studies that differentiate between OECD and non-OECD countries tend to find evidence of an environmental Kuznets curve for the first group of countries but not for the second. Although many developed countries now require environmental assessments of trade agreements that they enter into, these assessments tend to be focused on national rather than cross-border or global pollutants. A few of these assessments have raised concerns about the possible increase in greenhouse gas emissions from increased transport activity, although none have attempted a detailed quantitative analysis of these effects. Some assessments have alluded to the potential of mitigation measures to reduce the effects of increased emissions from transport.

From the evidence that has been gathered to date, studies on whether or not there is an environmental Kuznets curve for greenhouse gas emissions have produced conflicting results, as Huang *et al.* (2008) note. Holtz-Eakin and Selden (1995) examined data on 130 countries for the years 1951 to 1986, with complete sets of data for 108 of these countries. They are able to estimate an environmental Kuznets curve for $CO_2$ emissions, but find that it differs from the curve for local pollutants (pollutants that are confined within local or national borders) in that the turning point—at which further income growth leads to lower emissions—occurs only at very high income levels. Roberts and Grimes (1997) looked at a larger sample of countries (147 countries) and a longer time period (1962-91). They find that the relationship between $CO_2$ emissions per unit of GDP and level of economic development has changed from essentially linear in 1962 (i.e. each change in GDP and in level of economic development gave rise to a constant amount of change in $CO_2$ emission levels), to strongly curvilinear in 1991 (in other words, the amount of change in emission levels became larger and larger in response to each change in GDP and economic development level). They also find that, during a brief period in the early 1970s, and increasingly since 1982, the environmental Kuznets curve reached statistical significance. They conclude, however, that this is not the result of groups of countries passing through stages of development, but is due to improvements in production efficiency in a small number of developed countries, combined with reduced efficiency in low and middle-income countries. The study by

McCarney and Adamowicz (2005) which was discussed above also estimates an environmental Kuznets curve for $CO_2$ emissions, with the turning point being found at lower levels of per capita income in autocratic countries as compared to democratic ones. This result suggests that emissions would begin declining at lower levels of income in autocratic countries compared to more democratic countries. Other empirical studies find no environmental Kuznets curve for greenhouse gas emissions. The World Bank (1992) finds that per capita $CO_2$ emissions always increase with income. The study by Shafik (1994) shows that although some environmental indicators (such as water and sanitation) improve with rising incomes, others (such as particulates and sulphur oxides) initially deteriorate before eventually improving, while othersbecome steadily worse (carbon dioxide emissions,dissolved oxygen in rivers and municipal solid wastes, for example).

Moomaw and Unruh (1997) identify 16 countries (a subset of OECD members) that demonstrate sustained income growth with stable or decreasing levels of $CO_2$ emissions per capita. Using these 16 countries, they then compare two models—an environmental Kuznets curve and what they term a structural transition model of per capita $CO_2$ emissions and per capita GDP—to see which model best matches the experience of these 16 countries. The structural transition model attempts to find a sudden change in the pattern of the data and relate it to some precipitating event. They find that improvements in levels of $CO_2$ emissions per capita are not correlated with income levels, but are closely linked with historic events related to the oil-price shocks of the 1970s and to the policies that followed. They conclude that an environmental Kuznets curve for $CO_2$ emissions and income does not provide a reliable indication of future behaviour. Using more recent data from the period 1990 to 2003, Huang *et al.* (2008) test for the existence of an environmental Kuznets curve for greenhouse gas emissions in transition economies and (Kyoto Protocol) Annex II countries. They conclude that the evidence for most of these countries does not support the environmental Kuznets curve hypothesis. The Frankel and Rose (2005) study is also unable to find an environmental Kuznets curve for $CO_2$ emissions. There is also within-country studies. Aldy (2005) analyzes state-level $CO_2$ emissions in the United States from 1960 to 1999, and is able to estimate production-based $CO_2$ environmental Kuznets curves and consumption-based $CO_2$ environmental Kuznets curves. But in testing the robustness of these Trade and Climate Change relationships, he finds that estimated environmental Kuznets curves appear to vary by state. Furthermore, in some states with non-stationary income and emissions data (data whose statistical properties vary with time), he concludes that the estimated relationship between income and emission levels does not accurately reflect the true situation.

The "environmental Kuznets curve" (as this inverted U-shaped relationship between environmental quality and income has been called) has generated a great deal of research interest. Much of the theoretical literature on this topic has attempted to explain the nature and causes of this non-linear relationship between per capita income and environmental quality. The explanations have been varied. Some have alluded to indivisibilities in technologies, which means that below a certain threshold of income only polluting technologies are used, while cleaner technologies are used only when income rises above that threshold (Stokey, 1998). Some attribute the non-linearity between income and environmental quality to the fact that pollution is generated by consumption while there are increasing "returns to scale" in abatement, which implies that abatement of pollution becomes more efficient as an economy becomes richer (Andreoni and Levinson, 2001). Still other explanations ascribe the environmental Kuznets curve to the presence of pollution stock externalities, which means that if the stock of pollution depreciates quickly the net benefits from pollution control will rise with income (Kelly, 1997). While others, still, have described it as a consequence of developed countries exporting their older, more pollution-intensive technologies to developing countries (Suri and Chapman, 1998). In terms of political economy, the presence of advanced collective decision-making institutions (such as representative democracy) in developed countries and the absence of such institutions in some developing countries may explain this inverted U-shaped relationship (Jones and Manuelli, 1995). However, the "environmental Kuznets curve" might not be applicable to global pollution. Since greenhouse gas emissions are released into the "global commons" (the atmosphere), and part of their cost is therefore borne by people in other countries, there would not be a strong incentive for nations to take action to reduce such emissions, even if their citizens' incomes were improving. Since the scale effect and the technique effect tend to work in opposite directions, and the composition effect depends on the countries' "comparative advantage" and on the pollution-haven hypothesis, the overall impact of trade on greenhouse gas emissions cannot be easily determined. The answer will depend on the magnitude or strength of each of the three effects, and determining these will require detailed analysis of empirical evidence. Finally, although the literature on this subject has not touched on the timing of these effects, it is possible to hazard a few remarks on the issue.

First, how quickly these effects occur will depend on how rapidly trade opening measures are implemented and how far-reaching they are. Bilateral agreements or free trade agreements generally involve deeper commitments and more accelerated time-frames than multilateral agreements. Despite this, some studies have found that most bilateral or free trade agreements only manage to liberalize 90 per cent of their tariff lines for goods by the tenth year of implementation. There may also be politically sensitive sectors where these periods span more than a decade. Second, the reallocation of resources within an economy in response to the removal of trade barriers may be subject to adjustment costs. The extent to which governments reduce these adjustment costs through retraining of workers and provision of job search assistance will determine how smoothly this reallocation of resources takes place. Thus, while it is possible that the scale, composition and technique effects will be discernible in the first year of implementation of a trade agreement, it is more likely that it may be many years later before they become fully apparent.

### (c) Environmental Assessments of Trade Agreements

The environmental assessments of trade agreements that have been undertaken by countries engaged in negotiating multilateral and bilateral free trade agreements are another possible source of information on the expected impact of trade on greenhouse gas emissions. Negotiations under the Doha Round are still ongoing, but a large number of other free trade agreements have been negotiated and come into force over the past two decades. The WTO has been notified of 243 regional trade agreements (RTAs) which are currently in force.

A significant number of the agreements that were concluded during the current decade have been the subject of formal environmental assessments. Among WTO members, Canada, the European Communities and the United States have required environmental assessments of the trade agreements that they have entered into. A WTO report (2007) provides an inventory of the environmental assessments that have been notified to the WTO's Committee on Trade and Environment. Before examining the results of these assessments, it may be helpful to consider their limitations. First, nearly all of these assessments involve an analysis of the likely economic, environmental, and frequently also social, impacts of the trade agreements. As such, the conclusions reached by the studies, if any, are about the anticipated rather than actual impacts of the trade agreements. Only a few of the environmental assessments analyze climate change impacts; most deal with local or domestic environmental impacts. This may be because a study of climate change impacts was not included in the scope of the assessment, or because the impact the trade agreement would have on greenhouse gas emissions was considered to be negligible. Furthermore, although some of the assessments apply the scale, composition and technique effect framework, few are able to provide quantitative estimates of the impact each of these effects would have as a result of the trade agreement. Despite their limitations, these studies nonetheless offer some insights into the issues that have been of concern to trade negotiators and civil society groups as they examine specific trade agreements for their likely environmental impacts. Of the environmental assessments, those for the Australia-US Free Trade Agreement, the EU-Chile Free Trade Agreement, the EU-Mercosur Association Agreement, the Euro-Mediterranean Free Trade Area and the North American Free Trade Agreement consider their consequences on climate change. Both Australia and the United States conducted their own environmental assessments of the Australia-US Free Trade Agreement. While the United States' environmental review did not look at climate change, the Australian study concluded that the free trade agreement would entail a significant increase in domestic and international transportation, which would result in an increase in greenhouse gas emissions, as well as in other pollution (Cebon, 2003). NAFTA is probably the trade agreement that has received the most intensive scrutiny. The North American Commission on Environmental Cooperation, an institution which was established by NAFTA, has produced or commissioned a large number of environmental studies. Several of these have discussed the effects of NAFTA on greenhouse gas emissions. The North American Symposium on Assessing the Linkages between Trade and Environment is a collection of 13 studies on the environmental effects of NAFTA. One of the papers, "NAFTA Transportation Corridors: Approaches to Assessing Environmental Impacts and Alternatives", has managed to assess, in some detail, the greenhouse gas emissions arising from trucking and rail freight of trade within the NAFTA region (CEC, 2002). North American goods move by a variety of means-highways, railways, waterways, air and pipeline—but trucking and rail freight were judged to produce the most greenhouse gas emissions and to pose the greatest risk to air quality. Several of the main transport routes (or "transport corridors") for NAFTA trade were selected for the analysis: Vancouver-Seattle, Winnipeg-Fargo, Toronto-Detroit, San Antonio-Monterrey and Tucson-Hermosillo. The study determined the current and anticipated future commodity flows, freight vehicle traffic volumes, and levels of emissions for each of these transport corridors. A range of air pollution emissions, including greenhouse gas emissions, were also examined. The study's main conclusion is that trade-related emissions of greenhouse gases are expected to rise substantially by 2020. Using estimated growth by the year 2020 as a basis for comparison, it was calculated that the carbon dioxide emissions from NAFTA trade would increase by 2.4 to 4 times over their current levels in the five corridors. However, the study points to opportunities to achieve lower levels of trade-related emissions through the implementation of mitigation strategies. For example, reducing empty-vehicle mileage (by ensuring that vehicles carrying goods from one point to another made their return journey carrying a different cargo) would lower all pollutant emissions from trade. Based on the analysis of the Toronto-Detroit corridor, reducing the fraction of empty trucks from 15 per cent to 10 per cent would eliminate over 0.5 metric tonnes of nitrogen oxide and 600 metric tonnes of carbon dioxide per day by 2020 (5 per cent of the trade-related truck total). The study suggests that the main US-Mexico transport corridors have the potential for even larger reductions through the implementation of a similar mitigation strategy. Several studies completed in 1999 also discuss greenhouse gas emissions from various sectors where NAFTA was expected to have a significant impact (CEC, 1999b, 1999c, 1999d). A study of "feedlot" cattle (i.e. cattle being fattened for consumption) identified methane emissions from cattle as being an environmental concern. It concludes that although methane emissions remain a challenge, increased efficiency in beef-feeding, combined with genetic selection of the beef herd, could reduce total methane emission levels.

A second study focused on the electricity-generation sector in NAFTA countries, but also included the industries further up the supply chain that provide the major fuel sources used for electricity generation (notably coal, natural gas and hydroelectric installations) in its analysis. It concludes that the environmental pressures arising from increased demand for and trade in electricity in Canada, Mexico and the United States will depend on two key factors: the domestic environmental regulations imposed on the operation of existing power plants; and the impact of new electricity-generation technologies on fuel production. The EU's environmental assessment of the EU-Chile Free Trade Agreement did not address this agreement's overall impact on greenhouse gas emissions. However, it did examine the effect of the agreement on the forestry sector, where commercial operation has been increasingly based on forest plantations. The assessment anticipated that growth in demand for forest products would be met by products obtained from plantations. It concluded that these plantations could slow down climate change by capturing carbon dioxide, thus contributing to the reduction of carbon dioxide concentrations in the atmosphere. With regard to the Euro-Mediterranean Free Trade Agreement, the EU assessment indicated an overall adverse impact on climate change, due both to the increase in greenhouse gas emissions from increased transport and to changes in consumption patterns in the Mediterranean partner countries. It noted that the scale effect—which arises from increased trade and subsequent increases in production and consumption—can, in principle, be countered by technology or by regulation. However, it did not analyse any measures to strengthen the positive effects so as to counteract the adverse ones. The assessment did, however, indicate that the free trade agreement would give rise to an overall economic gain, a part of which, it suggested, could be directed towards measures to mitigate the expected climate change impacts. As part of its sustainability impact assessment of trade agreements, the EU examined the likely impact of an EU-Mercosur Association Agreement (University of Manchester, 2007), and concluded that the impacts of the proposed trade agreement on climate change are mixed. There would be a small reduction in greenhouse gas emissions from the reallocation of production between Mercosur and the EU. A free trade agreement could lead to less energy consumption during production because the energy-intensive parts of the manufacturing sector would be largely transferred to Europe where, in general, firms are more energy efficient than their Mercosur counterparts. The lower energy consumption and increased use of natural gas would lead to a small downturn in the total carbon dioxide emissions from production in both Mercosur countries and in the EU. However, the study concluded that this would be countered by a larger increase in carbon dioxide emissions arising from the increase in international transport. Overall, the association agreement could lead to an increase in global $CO_2$ emissions of about 0.15 per cent as a result of the full liberalization of agriculture and of manufactured goods.

### (d) Other Approaches

Instead of calculating the impact of trade opening on greenhouse gas emissions, some studies have tried to account for the contribution of international trade to $CO_2$ emissions. Peters and Hertwich (2008a, 2008b), for example, have suggested that 21.5 per cent of global $CO_2$ emissions are a result of international trade. Similar studies have been undertaken by the Stockholm Environment Institute and the University of Sydney to estimate the $CO_2$ emissions associated with UK trade (Wiedmann *et al.*, 2007). What these studies have in common is that they calculate emissions associated with consumption rather than those resulting from production. Since consumption, by definition, involves trade (consumption = production + imports—exports), it is necessary to estimate the $CO_2$ emissions "embodied" in trade. (In practice, the studies use emissions from the production of these traded goods to calculate the emissions "embodied" in trade.) However, these estimates do not imply that halting international trade would eliminate 21.5 per cent of greenhouse gas emissions, since domestic products would take the place of imported products. These would in themselves be a source of emissions. Studies employing the same approach, but applied to specific countries or pairs of trade partners, have also been undertaken by McGregor *et al.* (2008), who estimate the amount of $CO_2$ emissions contained in trade between Scotland and the rest of the United Kingdom; by Shui and Harriss (2006), who focus on the $CO_2$ emissions embodied in US-China trade; and by Sanchez-Choliz and Duarte (2004), who examine the $CO_2$ emissions embodied in Spain's international trade.

## Section III

## TRADE AND TRANSPORT

One important issue concerning trade's role in greenhouse gas emissions is its link to transportation services. International trade involves countries specializing in the production and export of goods where they have a comparative advantage and importing other goods from their trade partners where they have no such advantage. This process of international exchange requires that goods be transported from the country of production to the country of consumption, and consequently an expansion in international trade is likely to lead to increased use of transportation services. Merchandise trade can be transported by air, road, rail and water, or via pipelines in the case of oil. In most instances, international trade in merchandise will involve more than one mode of transport, since even goods that are carried by air or by water must often make an overland journey to the seaport or airport, and are generally transported by land on the final stretch of their journey to the ultimate consumer. At a global level, maritime transport accounts for the bulk of international trade transport by volume, and for a significant share by value. Excluding intra-EU trade, the United Nations Conference on Trade and Development (UNCTAD) (2007b) reported that, in 2006, seaborne cargo accounted for 89.6 per cent of world trade transport by volume; overland and other modes of transport (including pipelines) accounted for another 10.2 per cent; while airborne cargo accounted for the remaining 0.27 per cent . By value, seaborne trade made up 70.1 per cent of global trade transport, airborne cargo accounted for 14.1 per cent, and land and other modes of transport for the remaining 15.8 per cent.28 Since 2000, the share by volume of each of these modes of transport appears to have changed very little, with the share of maritime transport remaining almost invariable at 89 per cent. The share by value, however, has been more subject to change, with maritime transport's share varying between 64 and 70 per cent. The inclusion of trade within the EU changes the picture somewhat. Lloyd's Maritime Intelligence Unit (MIU) estimated that seaborne trade accounted for 76.5 per cent of international trade transport by volume and air transport for 0.3 per cent, while the share of overland transport was 15.9 per cent and that of pipelines was 7.3 per cent. By value, the share of seaborne cargo represented 58 per cent of the total, air cargo 11 per cent, overland cargo 39 per cent and transport via pipelines accounted for 2 per cent. The apparent reduction in the share of maritime transport can be explained by the fact that only a small proportion—18.1 per cent (by volume)—of trade within the EU is transported by sea although 71.7 per cent of its trade with the rest of the world is by sea (OECD, 2006a).

At the regional level, there is of course considerable variation in the importance of the various modes of transport. Countries that share a land border will have a greater share of trade being transported by land. Hummels (2007) estimates that in North America, nearly 25 to 35 per cent of trade by value is transported by land. The OECD (2006a) estimates that, in 2004, 31.1 per cent of trade within the EU was transported by road, another 6.1 per cent by rail and 7.7 per cent by pipeline. The role of international trade in increasing greenhouse gas emissions caused by road transport has been highlighted in a number of environmental assessments of regional trade agreements such as NAFTA (these assessments were reviewed in the previous sub-section). By contrast, for countries in Africa, the Middle East and Asia, only between 1 and 5 per cent of trade by value is with neighbouring countries, and thus the bulk of trade is carried by sea or by air. While the greater part of international trade is transported by sea, the volume of goods shipped by air (tonnes/kilometre) has been growing rapidly: between 1951 and 2004, it grew at 11.7 per cent annually –about twice the rate of other modes of world trade transport. This comparatively faster increase in the use of air transport for the shipment of goods can be explained by technological improvements (e.g. the invention and widespread use of the jet engine) which have resulted in a sharp decline in the cost of air shipping; by a fall in the value-to-weight ratio of manufactured goods; and by the growing importance of speed in international trade (Hummels, 2007). With the exception of diesel motor vehicles, however, aviation is the most polluting mode of transport for the movement of both passengers and freight (Chapman, 2007), and this may pose an increasingly important challenge, since the use of aviation services to convey internationally traded goods is likely to grow faster than the use of other modes of transport. Petroleum supplies 95 per cent of the total energy used by world transport, so the transport sector is a significant source of greenhouse gas emissions.[31] There are significant differences, however, in the contribution of the various modes of transport to energy-related greenhouse gas emissions. A recent report by the Intergovernmental Panel on Climate Change (IPCC) (Kahn Ribeiro *et al.*, 2007) estimated that about 74 per cent of the energy-related $CO_2$ emissions of the transport sector, including the carriage of both goods and people, was produced from road transport, with another 12 per cent from air transport.[32] It should be noted that, since only emissions that arise from international trade are being considered here, these numbers will overestimate the contribution of these two modes of transport, as they include emissions produced during the transport of people. In the case of maritime transport, the International Maritime Organization (IMO) has recently completed its study of $CO_2$ emissions of ships (IMO, 2008).[33] The report covers several elements: (i) an inventory of current emissions of $CO_2$ from international shipping (defined as merchant ships above 100 gross tonnes (GT)[34] in size); (ii) a comparison of the $CO_2$ emissions from various types of ships with the $CO_2$ emissions from other sources in the transport sector; and (iii) estimates of future emissions of $CO_2$ from international shipping. For 2007, the IMO study estimates the $CO_2$ emissions from international shipping to be about 843 million tonnes of $CO_2$, which is 2.7 per cent of the total world $CO_2$ emissions generated by human activity. The IMO study also compares the "carbon emission efficiency" index (which the IMO defined as $CO_2$ efficiency = $CO_2$/tonne-kilometre) of ships with that of other modes of transport. The lower this index, the more carbon-emission efficient a mode of transport is. It found that shipping has the lowest value of the index among the different modes of transport. The study also compares the share of each mode of transport in the sector's total $CO_2$ emissions and arrives at figures similar to those given by the IPCC report (Kahn Ribeiro *et al.*, 2007): road transport accounted for the biggest share of emissions, with 72.6 per cent, followed by international shipping with 11.8 per cent, then aviation with 11.2 per cent and finally rail transport, which accounted for 2 per cent. Finally, the study used the scenarios in the IPCC's Special Report on Emission Scenarios (SRES) to estimate future $CO_2$ emissions from international shipping. The IMO base scenario predicts that emissions from international shipping will increase from current levels by between 125.7 per cent and 218 per cent by the year

2050. The base scenario also predicts that increases over the next decade (to 2020) will range from a low of 9.7 per cent to a high of 25.5 per cent above current emission levels. The major part of international trade is transported by sea (90 per cent when calculated by weight and 70 per cent when calculated by value). This proportion appears to have remained steady, at least since 2000, despite the rapid growth in the use of air transport. Among the different modes of transport, shipping is also the most efficient in terms of carbon dioxide emissions. It is important to take this into account when assessing the contribution of trade to transport-related emissions. However, it should not be taken as a cause for complacency since there are warning signs that, without significant policy or regulatory changes, $CO_2$ emissions from international shipping will rise by significant amounts in the next four decades.

## SECTION IV

## TRADE AND ENVIRONMENT NEGOTIATIONS UNDER THE WTO

There have been significant overlaps between climate change and trade policies and intense negotiations at different international fora have taken place over the implications of multilateral interventions In the Marrakesh Agreement establishing the WTO, members highlighted a clear link between sustainable development and trade opening—in order to ensure that market opening goes hand in hand with environmental and social objectives. In the Doha Round of negotiations, members went further in their pledge to pursue a sustainable development path by launching the first-ever multilateral trade and environment negotiations. Decisions in these multilateral regimes—but also more broadly in regional, bilateral and national arenas—are likely to greatly influence the future of both international trade and the global climate. The use of trade-related measures has so far been eschewed under the UNFCCC or Kyoto Protocol, even if they have been used in other multilateral environmental agreements, such as the Montreal Protocol for the Protection of the Ozone Layer. Moreover, climate negotiators have typically avoided trade-related issues, preferring to defer these issues to the WTO. In a similar vein, the WTO has been very cautious in addressing climate change, often highlighting that such issues are more suitably decided within the climate change regime. At the level of principles, there have been some tensions as the climate regime's principle of "common but differentiated responsibilities" seemed at times difficult to reconcile with the rules and principles of trade law. The principle of "Common but differentiated responsibilities" calls for developed countries to cut their emissions first, while allowing developing countries additional carbon space to grow. According to this principle, countries will have to be treated differently, while the trade regime aims for an open and non-discriminatory trading system which treats all partners equally. Nonetheless , the regimes share a number of general principles, such as the endorsement of sustainable development, economic growth and an open international economy. These shared principles fit within the frame of the dominant neoliberal discourse of the early 1990s when both regimes emerged. The climate regime can be seen as a reflection of a "minimalist or default-approach to trade environment integration", a discourse that posits compatibility of climate protection, economic growth and trade liberalization. This discourse has helped to manage potential conflict between the regimes. According to Eckersley, when claiming that the WTO is undermining the climate regime, environmental non-governmental organizations tend to overlook that the principles of neoliberal environmentalism have in fact been endorsed by climate policy-makers when they adopted the UNFCCC in 1992. This "harmonious" relation may, however, come under pressure in the future, particularly if unilateral trade measures are adopted to address climate change challenges. At the multilateral level, a number of policies can be envisaged that would help to ensure trade supports climate change mitigation or, at a minimum, limit potential adverse impacts. As always in multilateral negotiations involving many countries, the principal challenge lies in developing rules that are acceptable to everyone, possibly as part of a larger package deal. Institutionally, the question is whether such rules should be developed and applied within the trade or the climate regime. Within the WTO, proposals for action include liberalization of trade in environmental goods and services (EGS), creating additional flexibilities under the Agreement on Trade-Related Aspects of Intellectual Property Rights to facilitate the transfer of low-carbon technologies, and a possible agreement defining the conditions when unilateral trade measures, such as border adjustment measures, would be acceptable. All of these areas might hold some potential, but cautions against overestimating their impact in terms of emissions reductions. Concerning the climate regime and its potential use of trade measures, an analogy is often made with the Montreal Protocol, which successfully used trade measures to support its implementation. Such an analogy can be misleading as the context for the ozone and climate regimes is fundamentally different. The scope of economic activities concerned and the amount of financing needed is much higher in the case of climate change. It will therefore be indispensable to mobilize massive investment in the climate sector and to remove barriers that currently inhibit such investment. A multilateral agreement on ways to promote such investment would be a difficult but rewarding way forward.

One issue addressed in the Doha Round is the relationship between the WTO and multilateral environmental agreements (MEAs), such as the UNFCCC. In this area of negotiations, WTO members have focused on opportunities for further strengthening cooperation between the WTO and MEA secretariats, as well as promoting coherence and mutual supportiveness between the international trade and environment regimes. While, to date, there have been no WTO legal disputes directly involving

MEAs, a successful outcome to the Doha negotiations will nevertheless contribute to reinforcing the relationship between the trade and environmental regimes. The negotiators have drawn from experiences in the negotiation and implementation of MEAs at the national level, and are seeking ways to improve national coordination and cooperation between trade and environment policies. Also in the context of the Doha Round, ministers have singled out environmental goods and services for liberalization. The negotiations call for "the reduction, or as appropriate, elimination of tariff and non-tariff barriers to environmental goods and services". The objective is to improve access to more efficient, diverse and less expensive environmental goods and services on the global market, including goods and services that contribute to climate change mitigation and adaptation. Climate-friendly technologies can be employed to mitigate and adapt to climate change in diverse sectors.

Many of these technologies involve products currently being discussed in the Doha negotiations, such as wind and hydropower turbines, solar water heaters, photovoltaic cells, tanks for the production of biogas and land fill liners for methane collection. In this context, the WTO environmental goods and services negotiations have a role to play in improving access to climate-friendly goods and technologies. There are two key rationales for reducing tariffs and other trade-distorting measures in climate-friendly goods and technologies. First, reducing or eliminating import tariffs and non-tariff barriers in these types of products should reduce their price and therefore facilitate their deployment. The access to lower-cost and more energy-efficient technologies may be particularly important for industries that must comply with climate change mitigation policies (see Part IV). Second, liberalization of trade in climate-friendly goods could provide incentives and domestic expertise for producers to expand the production and export of these goods. Trade in climate-friendly goods has seen a considerable increase in the past few years, including exports from a number of developing countries.

The Marrakech Agreement establishing the World Trade Organization was concluded two years after the Earth Summit, but apart from a general endorsement of sustainable development in the preamble, there has been no fundamental changes to the basic principles of the GATT to bring them into alignment with the Rio Declaration's principles of sustainable development. For instance, neither the precautionary principle nor the principle of "common but differentiated responsibilities" were mentioned in the WTO Agreements. However, the pivotal moment that set the shape of the relationship between the climate and trade regimes occurred not in 1994, when the Marrakech Agreement was signed, but rather in 1992 when the UNFCCC was concluded and signed. Rather than push for the recalibration of the international trade rules to conform with the requirements of climate protection, or push for the use of trade measures to enforce compliance and ensure fairness to "first movers" in the climate regime, the Parties to the climate regime have ensured that liberalized trade and an expanding global economy have been protected against trade restrictive climate policies.

## Section V

## CONTRIBUTION OF TRADE AND TRADE OPENING TO MITIGATION AND ADAPTATION EFFORTS

The technique effect can be a major mechanism through which trade opening can lead to mitigation of climate change. More open trade can increase the availability of goods and services that are more energy efficient. The increased income made possible through trade opening can lead to greater demand for better environmental quality and thus to reduced greenhouse gas emissions. Related to this, trade (or trade opening) encourages the spread from one country to another of technological innovations that are beneficial in mitigating climate change. Furthermore, allowing international markets to remain open could help countries adapt to supply disruptions that may be triggered by climate change, such as a shortage in food supplies.

### (a) Technological Spillovers from Trade

International trade can serve as a means for diffusing new technologies and know-how (Grossman and Helpman, 1991). International technology diffusion is important because of the highly skewed distribution of spending on research and development (R&D) around the world. Coe, Helpman and Hoffmaister (1997) estimate that 96 per cent of global expenditure on R&D is undertaken by only a handful of industrialized countries. The distribution of expenditure on R&D is even more skewed than the distribution of world income. Keller (2004) notes that the G-7 countries (the world's leading industrialized countries) accounted for 84 per cent of global spending on R&D in 1995, but represented only 64 per cent of global gross domestic product (GDP). Since Solow (1956), economists have understood the importance of technological change in raising productivity and underpinning economic growth. The greater a country's exposure to the international economy, the more it gains from R&D activities in other countries (Helpman, 1997). This suggests a similar role for trade in diffusing technologies that mitigate climate change. The available information indicates that 90 per cent of what is termed the environmental goods and services industry is located in member-countries of the OECD. Since many OECD countries were among the first to adopt climate change mitigation measures, the already lopsided distribution of technological know-how may become more distorted as the adoption of mitigation measures leads to further innovation in environmental technologies in OECD countries. Porter and van der Linde (1995) have argued that domestic firms' compliance with environmental regulations can trigger technological innovations, since such inventions will lower firms' cost of compliance. The existence of spillovers in climate change technology (i.e. transfers of technological know-how from one country to another) provides one mechanism by which developing countries' own efforts to combat climate change can benefit from innovations in OECD countries. Section III.B provides information on trade opening in goods that may mitigate greenhouse gas emissions. There are several channels by which technological dissemination through trade can occur (Grossman and Helpman, 1991; Helpman, 1997). As explained in Section I.B.4(a), one channel is through the importation of innovations embodied in both intermediate goods (i.e. manufactured or processed goods which are used in further production processes) and capital goods (e.g. machinery or equipment used in the production of other goods and services) which a country could not have produced on its own. A second channel is through the transfer of knowledge about new production methods and design from developed countries. Third, international trade can increase the available opportunities for adapting foreign technologies to meet local conditions. Lastly, the learning opportunities arising from international economic relations will reduce the cost of future innovation and imitation, making them more accessible to developing countries.Th e literature examining evidence of the link between international trade and the dissemination of technology has looked at both trade in intermediate goods (Coe and Helpman, 1995) and trade in capital goods (Xu and Wang, 1999; Eaton and Kortum, 2001). There is also some work based on patent applications that examines how foreign technology is acquired by firms. It shows that contacts with foreigners in the form of trade and foreign direct investment facilitate the transfer of foreign technology (Globerman *et al.*, 2000). A survey by Keller (2004) and Acharya and Keller (2007) of the literature on this subject concludes that imports play a significant role in the international dissemination of technology. Sijm *et al.* (2004) surveyed the literature on the ways that technological know-how is transferred from one country to another. They argue that the technological know-how in Kyoto Protocol Annex I countries has a positive impact on non-Annex I countries, given that technology and know-how are transferred through foreign trade and through education. However, the authors also point out that this has not been quantified in a reliable manner. This suggests a fruitful avenue for future research: empirical studies that document the extent of such spillovers and the role that trade plays in the international diffusion of climate change technologies.

### (b) Trade as a Means of Economic Adaptation to Climate Change

Climate change threatens to disrupt the conditions under which a wide range of goods and services that are important to economic well-being are produced and consumed. Trade may increase the vulnerability to climate change of some countries because it leads them to specialize in the production of products in which they have a comparative advantage, while relying on imports to meet their requirements for other goods and services. These countries may become vulnerable if climate change leads to an interruption in their supply of imported goods and services. However, trade can also provide a means to bridge the differences in demand and supply conditions, so that if climate change leads to a scarcity of certain goods and services in a country, it will nonetheless be able to obtain what it needs from countries where these goods and services continue to be available. Thus, beyond mitigation, trade can play a valuable role in helping humankind adapt to the consequences of a warmer future.

Climate change is likely to affect agricultural production in a significant manner. Without trade, countries facing changed climatic conditions and lower crop yields will confront huge challenges in providing adequate supplies of food and agricultural raw materials to their populations. International trade allows the world to cushion the severity of climate change impacts on global agriculture by making it possible for a country to draw upon its trade partners' supplies to meet part of the demand for food and agricultural raw materials. But the extent to which international trade can play this buffering role depends on how economic scarcity or abundance are transmitted in terms of changes in prices across markets (i.e. agricultural prices rising in response to scarcity or falling in situations of abundance). Where prices are distorted by the use of certain trade measures, the contribution that trade can make in helping countries to adapt to climate change may be significantly reduced. If, as mentioned earlier, a country becomes vulnerable to climate change impacts because it has specialized in certain sectors of production (in the case, for example, of a country which specializes in mining, or in the manufacture of automobile parts, but which has a very small agricultural sector), matters will only deteriorate if its partners restrict trade to safeguard their own supplies. A number of economic studies have simulated how trade might help reduce the cost of adapting to climate change in the agricultural or food sectors. Reilly and Hohmann (1993) used the SWOPSIM (Static World Policy Simulation Model) of world food markets to simulate the effect of a range of climate change scenarios while allowing countries to partly adjust to these impacts through trade. Their scenarios assumed reductions in yield of between 10 and 50 per cent in the US, Canada and the European Communities, and assumed either increases or no change in yield in high-latitude regions (former Soviet Union, Northern Europe, China, Japan, Australia, Argentina, Brazil) and the rest of the world. They find that, even under the assumption of large reductions in food yields, the losses in economic welfare are small relative to GDP (a few hundredths to a few tenths of a per cent) for all the countries identified in the study. The study also finds that Australia and China would experience large net gains (between 2 and 6 per cent of their GDP). Their results illustrate the importance of international trade in promoting interregional adjustments in production and consumption and hence in lowering the costs from climate change.

The study by Rosenzweig *et al.* (1993) considers the effect that further liberalization in agricultural trade would have on the world's ability to adapt to climate change. The potential variations due to climate change in the yield of some major crops (wheat, rice, maize, and soybeans) were estimated. A number of climate change scenarios were considered in estimating these changes in yields, based on the assumption of a doubling in $CO_2$ levels (to 555 parts per million) by 2060. Three general circulation models (GCMs)—sophisticated computer models incorporating detailed observations of various weather phenomena and other factors, which are used to study past, present and future climate patterns—were employed to obtain a range of these climate change scenarios. The GCMs employed were from the Goddard Institute for Space Studies, the Geophysical Fluid Dynamics Laboratory and the United Kingdom Meteorological Office. These projected changes in yields were then fed into a world food trade computer model—the Basic Linked System (BLS)—and projections of the world food market up to 2060 were generated. The study finds that, with trade opening, global impacts due to climate changewould be slightly reduced. Price increases would be slightly less than those that would occur without full trade opening, and the number of people at risk from hunger would be reduced by about 100 million (from the reference case of about 640 million in 2060). The study by Hertel and Randhir (2000) continues this focus on trade policies in the agricultural sector and how they may affect adaptation to climate change. The study underscores the importance of reducing or eliminating trade-distorting measures, such as subsidies, so as to make international trade a more effective tool for adapting to climate change. Scenarios where international trade helps a country to adapt to climate change all result in net increases in economic welfare at the global level. But international trade contributes more efficiently as a tool for economic adaptation when agricultural subsidies are eliminated. The global economic welfare gains are nearly six times greater when subsidies are completely eliminated, because large subsidies to agriculture exacerbate inefficiencies in the global agricultural system. However, other studies demonstrating that agricultural trade opening can increase greenhouse gas emissions should not be discounted. A recent paper by Verburg *et al.* (2008), for example, employs the Global Trade Analysis Project (GTAP) computable general equilibrium model, together with the Integrated Model to Assess the Global Environment (IMAGE), to simulate the long-term consequences on global emission levels of removing all trade barriers in agriculture, particularly in the milk-livestock sector.

The study first establishes a baseline: the "business as usual" scenario. According to this baseline, by 2050, carbon dioxide ($CO_2$), methane and nitrous oxide ($N_2O$) emissions will be 63 per cent, 33 per cent and 20 per cent higher, respectively, than their levels in 2000. The authors simulate various trade opening scenarios. Full agricultural trade opening would add an extra 50 per cent of $CO_2$ emissions to the baseline scenario by 2015. This initial increase in emissions would, however, decrease over time, so that $CO_2$ emissions in 2050 would be 30 per cent lower compared to the baseline. Full liberalization would lead to an additional 1.7 per cent of $N_2O$ emissions by 2015, but this would later fall, so that by 2050 $N_2O$ emissions would be equal to the baseline. Methane is the only emission which would have increased, by an extra 5 per cent over the baseline level, in 2050. Despite these complicated evolutions over time, the authors suggest that the full liberalization scenario would lead to a small overall increase in greenhouse gases by 2050. Given the uncertainties about the impact of climate change on yields across regions and the long timescales involved in these simulations, the results of these studies should not by any means be seen as forecasts or predictions. Nevertheless, they serve to underline the means by which international trade can assist economies to adjust to changes which may occur in the inter-regional location of agricultural production as a result of climate change.

### (c) Possible Impact of Climate Change on Trade

So far, the discussion has been about how trade can affect greenhouse gas emissions, help mitigate climate change, or assist countries in adapting to future warming. But the link between trade and climate change is not only in one direction, since the physical processes associated direction, since the physical processes associated with climate change can also affect the pattern and volume of international trade flows. There appear to be two likely effects of climate change on international trade. First, climate change may alter countries' comparative advantages and lead to shifts in the pattern of international trade. This effect will be stronger on those countries whose comparative advantage stems from climatic or geophysical reasons. Countries or regions that are more reliant on agriculture may experience a reduction in exports if future warming and more frequent extreme weather events result in a reduction in crop yields. Warming need not always produce negative impacts on exports, since it may succeed in increasing agricultural yields in other regions. These climate change effects will not necessarily be confined to trade in merchandise goods but might extend to trade in services as well. Many tourist destinations rely on natural assets—beaches, clear seas, tropical climate, or abundant snowfall, for example—to attract holiday-makers. A rise in sea levels or changes in weather patterns might deprive countries of these natural assets. It could be argued, of course, that comparative advantage is never permanent. Technological breakthroughs, shifts in consumer preferences and changes in economic policies constantly buffet economies and alter the relative economic strengths of nations and overall competitiveness. Nevertheless, to the extent that climate change impacts may occur abruptly or that countries may be inadequately prepared, these adjustments can prove costly. In this context, international trade may become an important means of adapation. Second, climate change may increase the vulnerability of the supply, transport and distribution chains upon which international trade depends. The Fourth Assessment Report of the IPCC refers to some of these vulnerabilities (Wilbanks *et al.*, 2007a). Extreme weather events (such as hurricanes) may temporarily close ports or transport routes and damage infrastructure critical to trade. Transportation routes in permafrost zones may be negatively affected by higher temperatures, which would shorten the length of time that roads would be passable during winters. Coastal infrastructure and distribution facilities are vulnerable to flood damage. Transportation of bulk freight by inland waterways, such as the Rhine, could be disrupted during droughts. Disruptions to the supply, transport and distribution chains would raise the costs of undertaking international trade. While an increase in trade costs would be bad for trade in general, many developing countries whose integration into the global economy has depended on their participation in international production chains may be more vulnerable than developed .

Compared to the relationship between the WTO and the Cartagena Protocol on Biosafety, the relationship between the WTO and the Kyoto Protocol (and the broader climate regime) appears to be relatively harmonious and there has so far been no direct collision at the level of rules, and no instances of "forum shopping" by Parties with axes to grind. Yet this is not necessarily an indication that the two regimes are perfectly harmonized. While prescriptive rules are more or less unique to particular regimes, general principles (such as the polluter pays principle or the precautionary principle) and broader discourses (such as the "Washington consensus") are more ubiquitous and can form part of transnational discourses promoted by actors and organizations working across a range of policy networks and rule-making bodies. Policy discourses of economic and environmental integration, such as "sustainable development", represent specialized, transnational discourses that have become increasingly influential in shaping the way different economic and environmental regimes are interpreted and managed. The advantages of focusing on transnational policy discourses in the interplay between regimes is that it becomes possible to look for linkages or patterns in the discourses that are employed to construct and defend the principles and rules of different regimes. Discourses also shed light on the priority and weight given to particular principles and norms in legal texts. In effect, they determine which features of the regime are salient or operative and which are less important. A comparison of the principles of the two regimes reveals four significant points of overlap:

1. The endorsement of sustainable development—mentioned in the preamble of the Marrakech Agreement Establishing the WTO as well as in several articles of the United Nations Framework Convention on Climate Change (UNFCCC);
2. Special consideration of the circumstance of developing countries, although expressed in different language for different purposes—while the WTO regime includes provisions for "special and differential treatment", the climate regime has

endorsed the principle of "common but differentiated responsibilities";
3. Support for an open economic system including avoidance of any arbitrary or unjustifiable discrimination or disguised restrictions of trade—a principle inherent in the provisions of the trade regime, and explicitly Mentioned in Article 3.5 of the UNFCCC; and
4. The maintenance of economic growth—this is mentioned throughout the UNFCCC and basic to, though implicit, in the liberalization agenda of the WTO.

These are the principles that have received the most emphasis in the dominant "integration" discourse discussed below. However, there are also significant tensions among some of the non-overlapping principles. In particular, the UNFCCC principle of "common but differentiated responsibilities", which implies that developed countries take the lead in combating climate change on the basis of their greater historical responsibilities and capacity, sits uncomfortably with the trade regime's principles of non-discrimination and reciprocity which—if applied to the climate regime—would require tit for tat reductions in emissions without any positive discrimination or affirmative action in favour of developing countries to account for their development needs. Of course, the trade regime does make provision for the "special And differential treatment" of developing countries. However, the difference between "differential treatment" in the trade regime and "differentiated responsibilities" in the climate regime is key. While both regimes acknowledge differences in capacity and development needs, there is no sense in the trade regime that developed countries have a moral responsibility to pay a disproportionate share of the costs of collective action or "take the lead" on account of past actions; in this sense the climate regime provides a stronger challenge than the trade regime to the traditional principles of liberal contractualism, grounded in reciprocity, that formally underpin international treaty-making. This has significant implications for the emerging debate about the appropriateness of border adjustment measures (BAMs) to address the problem of carbon leakage, particularly if they were applied only to industrialized countries in deference to "common but differentiated responsibilities". Likewise, the climate regime's precautionary approach to risk could potentially justify a wide range of environmental regulations that might not be in conformity with the strictures of the WTO's rules on environmental exemptions.

### (d) The Interplay of Rules

The Kyoto Protocol remains faithful to the UNFCCC principle of avoiding arbitrary or unjustifiable discrimination or disguised restrictions on international trade by avoiding any explicit authorization of restrictive trade measures. This is despite the success of such measures in earlier multilateral environmental agreements, particularly in the fields of hazardous waste regulation, wildlife trade, and ozone protection. Indeed, Article 2.3 of the Kyoto Protocol takes this further in stipulating that the developed countries shall "strive to implement policies and measures under this Article in such a way as to minimize adverse effects, including . . . effects on international trade". Despite the absence of any direct conflict between the rules of the WTO and the Kyoto Protocol, there is nonetheless still considerable potential for conflict, depending on how Parties choose to implement their obligations. Thomas Brewer has identified 250 points of potential intersection between the five key operative provisions of the Protocol—international emissions trading, Clean Development Mechanism, and Joint Implementation, as well as compliance and domestic policy measures—and the 50 or so WTO agreements. However, the most significant area of potential intersection is the unilateral use of BAMs for imports or exports to address the problems of competitive disadvantage and possible "carbon leakage" arising from new national climate policies such as cap-and-trade schemes and/or carbon taxes. While the balance of legal opinion tends to suggest that appropriately designed and non-discriminatory unilateral BAMs are likely to be WTO-compatible, there is sufficient uncertainty to create the possibility of a legal challenge under the WTO's dispute settlement procedures. The problem with the BAM option is that the schemes that are most consistent with the objectives and principles of the climate regime (in respecting "common but differentiated responsibilities") are likely to be least consistent with the WTO rules. So, for example, an EU BAM scheme that would be directed only against US imports, as suggested by Joseph Stiglitz, or only against imports from developed countries with weak climate policies, would be likely to provoke a legal challenge in the WTO on the grounds that it is discriminatory, unless it can be justified as an environmental exemption under Article XX of the General Agreement on Tariffs and Trade (GATT). However, non-discriminatory BAMs would offend the principle of Northern leadership and "common but differentiated responsibilities" in the climate regime and can be expected to be strongly resisted by developing countries. Discourses operate at different levels of generality and specificity, from the local to the global, and from the highly technical to the everyday. Economic and environmental policy discourses represent specialized, transnational discourses that have become increasingly influential in shaping the way different regimes are interpreted and managed. Transnational discourses that have become hegemonic provide a means of stabilizing the meaning of the ideas, norms and procedures of regimes, and of framing and managing the relationship between overlapping regimes that might otherwise be in conflict.

## Counter-discourses on Trade and Climate Protection

The general claim that "trade liberalization generates wealth and innovation for climate protection" has been challenged by a range of environmental NGOs, green think tanks/research institutes, and academics working in the cognate fields of ecological economics and global political ecology. There is, of course, no single, unified NGO or academic view on the relationship between trade and climate protection. However, it is possible to draw together a generic counter-discourse,built on the elements and fragments of a variety of recurring counter-discourses about trade and environment in general, and trade and climate protection in particular, which provides a general counterpoint to the "winwin" discourse which selectively highlights the virtues of trade liberalization in EGS. These counter-arguments mostly acknowledge the benefits of removing distorting subsidies and liberalizing trade in EGS, but these areas of mutual synergy are considered minor when set against the more general consequences of trade liberalization that is not effectively disciplined by climate concerns. The core elements of this general counter-discourses are:

- the growing scale of trade following liberalization leads to rising aggregate greenhouse gas emissions and merely focusing on the additional transport costs of expanding trade misses this larger growth; reductions in the emissions intensity of production merely reduce the rate of the aggregate increase;
- trade leads to an "ecologically unequal exchange" (the North imports more materials, energy and bio-capacity that it exports) and therefore undermines environmental capacity in the South;
- the WTO's rules permit countries to use the environment as a "free resource"; the failure of the WTO to apply the polluter pays principle allows unfair subsidization; and
- the WTO's environmental exemptions are inadequate, and WTO rules undermine the climate regime by restricting the range of effective policy measures that can be used.

These contending discourses select and emphasize different elements of the standard economic framework for assessing the environmental effects of trade, which focuses on scale, composition, and technology effects and the environmental regulatory context, both internationally and domestically. In particular, the WTO discourse emphasizes the virtues of new technologies and the significance of the international environmental regulatory context, whereas the counter-discourses emphasize the problem of scale and composition (particularly, the relocation of emissions-intensive industry to developing countries). While the more general case for trade liberalization enjoys strong support within the discipline of neoclassical economics and among state elites, it has not always been thus. Despite the continuity in the principles of the GATT and the WTO, the international consensus about their meaning and application has evolved significantly since the 1940s. In broad outline, we have seen a shift from "embedded liberalism" of the immediate postwar period to the "Washington consensus" or "neoliberalism" of the 1980s, which has more or less prevailed through to the present, despite the debate about an emerging "post-Washington" consensus. Most noteworthy for the discursive explanation is that the rise of the new orthodoxy of neoliberalism in the 1980s coincided with the rise to prominence of the new global discourse of sustainable development.

In 1987, the Brundtland Report questioned the "limits-to-growth" discourse of the early 1970s by fundamentally challenging the idea that environmental protection and economic development stand in a simple zero-sum relationship. It became accepted that there is room for the development of virtuous synergies between economic growth (nationally and globally, via expanding world trade) and environmental protection. Of course, exactly how much room remains a matter of real contention, which has given rise to a spectrum of discourses of sustainable development and ecological modernization, ranging from "weak" (and merely technical) to "strong" (and comprehensive and reflexive) in terms of their likely efficacy in promoting lasting ecological sustainability. The discourse of sustainable development according to the Brundtland Report sits mid-way along this spectrum and argues that economic growth and environmental degradation can be "decoupled" through the pursuit of growth that uses less energy and natural resources, and produces less waste. It redefined limits in more flexible terms to encompass only the restrictions arising from "the state of technology and social organization on the environment's ability to meet present and future needs". Although the Brundtland Report stressed the winwin linkages between economic growth and environmental protection, it also sought to arrest the skewed distribution of global wealth and income and ensure the satisfaction of human needs, now and in the future. The Brundtland Report had offered a new synthesis of environment and development considerations that reflected a Keynesian-like compromise of "managed sustainable growth". However, by 1992, the Brundtland Report's discourse of sustainable development had been reinterpreted in more market-friendly terms to embrace the liberalization of trade and finance and the promotion of market policy tools over so-called "command-and-control" regulation. This provided the overarching "norm-complex" that was legitimated at the 1992 Earth Summit, encapsulated in the Rio Declaration, Agenda 21, the Convention on Biological Diversity and the UNFCCC. According to Bernstein, this more market-friendly discourse of liberal environmentalism only became institutionalized after the consolidation of neoliberalism and was therefore adapted to fit the new neoliberal frame. This explanation helps to shed light on the selective appropriation of the principles of the Rio Declaration by the Parties to the UNFCCC, including their conspicuous "deselection" of the polluter pays principle. Yet the polluter pays principle could have served as a useful integrating principle or lynchpin between the climate and trade regimes. It is conceptually consistent with the WTO's objective of removing unjustifiable subsidies in production, and could have provided a clear justification for BAMs. The polluter pays principle is also central to ensuring that energy prices reflect their full environmental and climate costs, consistent with the objectives of the climate regime.

## SECTION VI

## CONCLUDING OBSERVATIONS

The tremendous surge in world trade in recent years has raised the issue of the link between international trade and climate change induced greenhouse gas emissions. The task of national governments, particularly in developing world has been to devise strategies of trade and non-trade policies to combat and mitigate the ill-effects of trade induced climate change consequences for the growth process of these economies. The task is compounded by the international spillover effects of such emissions, and the multilateral framework of trade negotiations under the WTO. The issues of technological upgradation, financing of mitigation investments, role of FDI and the implications of tariff and non-tariff policies to protect the domestic environment from the trade engineered relations and emissions have been addressed in the recent literature on trade and climate change. It is realized that use of single instruments is insufficient to cope with the complex issues pertaining the link between forces of trade under the aegis of globalization and the environmental and related hazards that such activities lead to. A comprehensive multilateral approach based on cooperation between trading partners are needed. The issues of protectionism vs. free trade in an integrated world and the WTO's rule on environmental standards and the negotiations thereof call for a political economy approach, because of the minging of economic and political factors in such trade and climate change negotiations. The present essay highlights the main issues as gleaned through the literature to bring home the importance of such multi-disciplinary political economy approach to study the impact of trade on climate change and *vice versa* and derive policy rules to combat the challenges that lie ahead.

### REFERENCES

Acharya, R.C. and Keller, W. (2007), "Technology Transfer through Imports", *CEPR Discussion Paper* 6296, CEPR, London.

Aldy, J.E. (2005), "An Environmental Kuznets Curve Analysis of U.S. State-Level Carbon Dioxide Emissions", *Journal of Environment and Development,* 14:1, pp. 48-72.

Andreoni, J. and Levinson, A. (2001), "The Simple Analytics of the Environmental Kuznets Curve", *Journal of Public Economics,* 80:2, pp. 269-86.

Baldwin, R.E. (2000), "Trade and Growth: Still Disagreement about the Relationships", *Economics Department Working Paper,* 264, OECD, Paris.

CEC (1999a), *Issue Study 1. Maize in Mexico: Some Environmental Implications of the North American Free Trade Agreement(NAFTA).* Available at www.cec.org/fi les/pdf/ECONOMY/engfeed_EN.pdf.

CEC (1999b), *Issue Study 2. Feedlot Production of Cattle in the United States and Canada: Some Environmental Implications of the North American Free Trade Agreement (NAFTA).* Available at www.cec.org/fi les/pdf/ECONOMY/engfeed_EN.pdf.

CEC (1999c), *Issue Study 3. Electricity in North America: Some Environmental Implications of the North American FreeTrade Agreement (NAFTA).* Available at www.cec.org/fi les/pdf/ECONOMY/engelect_EN.pdf.

CEC (2002), *The Environmental Effects of Free Trade Papers Presented at the North American Symposium on Assessing the Linkages between Trade and Environment.* Available at www.cec.org/fi les/pdf/ECONOMY/symposium-e.pdf.

Chapman, L. (2007), "Transport and Climate Change:A Review", *Journal of Transport Geography,* 15, pp. 354-67.

Coe, D.T. and Helpman, R. (1995), "International R&D Spillovers", *European Economic Review* 39:5, pp. 859-87.

Coe, D.T., Helpman, E. and Hoffmaister, A. (1997), "North-South R&D Spillovers", *Economic Journal,* 107, pp. 134-49.

Copeland, B.R. and Taylor, M.S. (2003), *Trade and theEnvironment,* Princeton University Press, Princeton and Oxford.

Copeland, B.R. and Taylor, M.S. (2004), "Trade, Growth and the Environment", *Journal of Economic Literature,* 46:1, pp. 7-71.

Eaton, J. and Kortum, S. (2001), "Trade in Capital Goods", *European Economic Review* 45:7, pp. 1195-1235.

Edwards, S. (1998), "Openness, Productivity and Growth: What Do We Really Know?", *Economic Journal,* 108:1, pp. 383-98.

Frankel, J. and Rose, A. (2005), "Is Trade Good or Bad for the Environment? Sorting Out the Causality", *Review of Economics and Statistics,* 87:1, pp. 85-91.

Grether, J.M., Mathys, N.A. and de Melo, J. (2007), "Trade,Technique and Composition Effects: What is Behind the Fall in World-Wide $SO_2$ Emissions 1990-2000?", *Fondazione Enrico Mattei Nota Di Lavoro,* 93.

Globerman, S., Kokko, A. and Sjöholm, F. (2000), "Technology Sourcing in Swedish MNEs and SMEs: Evidence from Patent Data", *Kyklos* 53:1, pp. 17-38.

Grossman, G.M. and Helpman, E. (1991), *Innovation and Growth in the Global Economy,* MIT Press, Cambridge, MA, 375 p.

Grossman, G.M. and Krueger, A.B. (1993), "Environmental Impacts of a North American Free Trade Agreement", in Garber, P.M. (ed.), *The US-Mexico Free Trade Agreement,* MIT Press, Cambridge, MA, pp. 13-56.

Helpman, E. (1997), "R&D and Productivity: the International Connection", *National Bureau of Economic Research (NBER) Working Paper* 6101, Cambridge, Massachusetts.

Hertel, T. and Randhir, T. (2000), "Trade Liberalization as a Vehicle for Adapting to Global Warming", *Agriculture and Resource Economics Review,* 29:2, pp. 1-14.

Holz-Eakin, D., and Selden, T.M. (1995), "Stoking the Fires? $CO_2$ Emissions and Economic Growth", *Journal of Public Economics,* 57:1, pp. 85-101.

Huang, W.M., Lee, G.W.M. and Wu, C.C. (2008), "GHG Emissions, GDP Growth and the Kyoto Protocol: A Revisit of Environmental Kuznets Curve Hypothesis", *Energy Policy,* 36, pp. 239-47.

Hummels, D. (2007), "Transportation Costs and International Trade in the Second Era of Globalization", *Journal of Economic Perspectives,* 21:3, pp. 131-54.

Jones, L.E. and Manuelli, R.E. (1995), "A Positive Model of Growth and Pollution Controls", *Natiònal Bureau of EconomicResearch, Working Paper,* 5205.

Kahn Ribeiro, S., Kobayashi, S., Beuthe, M., Gasca, J., Greene, D., Lee, D.S., Muromachi, Y., Newton, P.J., Plotkin, S., Sperling, D., Wit, R., and Zhou, P.J. (2007), "Transport and Its Infrastructure", in Metz, B., Davidson, O.R., Bosch, P.R.

Dave, R. and Meyer, L.A. (eds.), *Climate Change 2007: Mitigation. Contribution of Working Group III to the Fourth Assessment Reportof the Intergovernmental Panel on Climate Change,* Cambridge University Press, Cambridge and New York, pp. 323-85.

Kelly, D.L. (1997), *On Kuznets Curves Arising from Stock Externalities,* Department of Economics Working Paper, University of California, Santa Barbara, CA. Keller, W. (2004), "International Technology Diffusion", *Journal of Economic Perspectives,* 42, pp. 752-82.

Managi, S. (2004), "Trade Liberalization and the Environment: Carbon Dioxide for 1960-1999", *Economics Bulletin,* 17:1, pp. 1-5.

Managi, S., Hibiki, A. and Tsurumi, T. (2008), "Does Trade Liberalization Reduce Pollution Emissions, *Research Institute of Economy, Trade and Industry (RIETI) Discussion Paper Series,* 08-E-013.

McCarney, G. and Adamowicz, V. (2005), *The Effects of Trade Liberalization on the Environment: An Empirical Study,* selected paper prepared for presentation at the Canadian Agricultural Economics Society Annual Meeting 6-8 July, San Francisco, California.

McGregor, P.G., Swales, K.K. and Turner, K. (2008), "The $CO_2$ 'Trade Balance' Between Scotland and the Rest of the UK: Performing a Multi-Region Environmental Input-Output Analysis with Limited Data", *Ecological Economics,* 66:4, pp. 662-73.

Moomaw, W.R. and Unruh, G.C. (1997), "Are Environmental Kuznets Curves Misleading Us? The Case of $CO_2$ Emissions", *Environment and Development Economics,* 2:4, pp. 451-63.

OECD (2004), *Current International Shipping Market Trends—Community Maritime Policy and Legislative Initiatives,* A paper presented at the OECD Workshop on Maritime Transport, OECD, Paris.

OECD (2005), *Trade that Benefits the Environment and Development: Opening Markets for Environmental Goods and Services,* OECD, Paris.

OECD (2006a), *Decoupling the Environmental Impacts of Transport from Economic Growth,* OECD, Paris.

OECD (2006b), *The Political Economy of Environmentally-related Taxes,* OECD, Paris, 199 p.

OECD (2008a), *Climate Change Mitigation: What do we do?,* OECD, Paris.

OECD (2008b), *OEGD Environmental Outlook to 2030,* OECD, Paris, 517 p.

OECD (2008c), *Promoting Sustainable Consumption: Good Practices in OECD Countries,* 59 p.

Peters, G.P. and Hertwich, E.G. (2008a), "$CO_2$ Embodied in International Trade with Implications for Global Climate Policy", *Environmental Science & Technology,* 42:5, pp. 1401-07.

Peters, G.P. and Hertwich, E.G. (2008b), "Post-Kyoto Greenhouse Gas Inventories: Production Versus Consumption", *Climatic Change*, 86, pp. 51-66.

Porter, M. and van der Linde, C. (1995), "Toward A New Conception of the Environment-Competitiveness Relationship", *Journal of Economic Perspectives*, 9:4, pp. 97-118.

Reilly, J. and Hohmann, N. (1993), "Climate Change and Agriculture: The Role of International Trade", *American Economic Review Papers and Proceedings*, 83:2, pp. 306-23.

Rodriguez, F. and Rodrik, D. (1999), "Trade Policy and Economic Growth: A Skeptic's Guide to the Cross-National Evidence", *NBER Working Paper*, 7081, NBER, Cambridge, MA.

Rosenzweig, C., Parry, M., Frohberg, K. and Fisher, G. (1993), *Climate Change and World Food Supply*, Oxford: Environmental Change Unit, University of Oxford.

Sachs, J.D. and Warner, A. (1995), "Economic Reform and the Process of Global Integration", *Brookings Papers on EconomicActivity*, 1995:1, pp. 1-95.

Shafik, N. (1994), "Economic Development and Environmental Quality: An Econometric Analysis", *Oxford Economic Papers*, 46, pp. 757-73.

Shui, B. and Harriss, R.C. (2006), "The Role of $CO_2$ Embodiment in US-China Trade", *Energy Policy*, 34:18, pp. 4063-4068.SIA-EMFTA Consortium (The European Union's Sustainability Impact Assessment Study of the Euro Mediterranean Free Trade Area) (2007), *Sustainability Impact Assessment of the Euro-Mediterranean Free Trade Area*. Available at http://trade.ec.europa.eu/doclib/docs/2006/november/tradoc_131340.pdf.

Sijm, J.P.M., Kuik, O.J., Patel, M., Oikonomou, V., Worrell, E., Lako, P., Annevelink, E., Nabuurs, G.J. and Elbersen, H.W.(2004), *Spillovers of Climate Policy: An Assessment of the Incidence of Carbon Leakage and Induced Technological Change due to $CO_2$ Abatement Measures*, ECN, Bilthoven.

Solow, R.M. (1956), "A Contribution to the Theory of Economic Growth", *Quarterly Journal of Economics*, 70:1, pp. 65-94.

Stokey, N.L. (1998), "Are there Limits to Growth?", *International Economic Review*, 39:1, pp. 1-31.

Suri, V. and Chapman, D. (1998), "Economic Growth, Trade and Energy: Implications For the Environmental Kuznets Curve", *Ecological Economics*, 25:2, pp. 195-208.

Torras, M. and Boyce, J. (1998), "Income, Inequality and Pollution", *Ecological Economics*, 25:2, pp. 147-60.

UNCTAD (2007), *UNCTAD Transport Newsletter*, 38, UNCTAD, Geneva.

Verburg, R., Woltjer, G., Tabeau, A., Eickhout, B. and Stehfest, E. (2008), *Agricultural Trade Liberalisation and Greenhouse Gas Emissions: A simulation Study Using the GTAP-IMAGE Modelling Framework*, LEI, The Hague.

UNEP (2009) : Climate And Trade Policies In a Post-2012 World, United Nations.

Wiedmann, T., Wood, R., Lenzen, M., Minx, J., Guan, D. and Barrett, J. (2007), *Development of an Embedded Carbon Emissions Indicator—Producing a Time Series of Input-Output Tables and Embedded Carbon Dioxide Emissions for the UK by Using a MRIO Data Optimisation System*, Report to the UK Department for Environment, Food and Rural Affairs by Stockholm Environment Institute at the University of York and Centre for Integrated Sustainability Analysis at the University.

Wilbanks, T.J., Leiby, P., Perlack, R., Ensminger, T.J. and Wright, S.B. (2007), *Toward an Integrated Analysis of Mitigation and Adaptation: Some Preliminary Findings, Mitigation and Adaptation Strategies for Global Change*, 12, pp. 713-25.

Wilbanks, T.J., Romero Lankao, P., Bao, M., Berkhout, F., Cairncross, S., Ceron, J.-P., Kapshe, M., Muir-Wood, R. and Zapata-Marti, R. (2007a), "Industry, Settlement and Society" in Parry, M.L., Canziani, O.F., Palutikof, J.P., van der Linden, P.J. and Hanson, C.E. (eds.), *Climate Change 2007: Impacts, Adaptation and Vulnerability. Contribution of Working Group II to the Fourth Assessment Report of the Intergovernmental Panel on Climate Change*, Cambridge University Press, Cambridge, pp. 357-90.

World Bank (1992), *The World Bank Development Report 1992: Development and the Environment*, The World Bank, Washington, DC.

WTO (2007), *List of Environmental Reviews*, WT/CTE/W/245, Note by the Secretariat, 21 p.

Xu, B. and Wang, J. (1999), "Capital Goods Trade and R&D Spillovers in the OECD", *Canadian Journal of Economics*, 32, pp. 1258-74.

# 3

# Natural Disaster, Risk and Insurance—An Analytical Review

## I. INTRODUCTION : CLIMATE CHANGE AND NATURAL DISASTER

Large sudden natural disasters such as earthquakes, tsunamis, hurricanes, and floods generate destructive impact. Recent events such as the Indian Ocean tsunami in 2004, hurricane Katrina in 2005, and the Haitian and Chilean earthquakes in 2010 have received worldwide media coverage, and there is an increasing sense of awareness among the general public about the destructive nature of disasters. Climate change is expected to increase the severity and frequency of weather-related natural hazards such as storms, high rainfalls, floods, droughts and heat-waves Coupled with sea level rise, this will lead to more disasters in future unless prompt action is taken. Over the period 1995-2004, a total of 2,500 million people were affected by disasters, with losses of 890,000 dead and US$ 570 billion costs. About 75% of natural disasters are related to weather extremes. Of particular concern is the fact that disasters have been increasing over recent decades, mainly owing to increased populations in hazard-prone locations, unplanned settlements and environmental degradation, but evidence is also mounting that climate change is a factor too, for example in more intense hurricanes, higher rainfall intensities and heat-waves.

The vast majority of people affected by natural disasters suffer from climate-related disasters. To be precise in estimates, between 1980 and 2007, 98% of all those affected by natural disasters suffered from climate-related ones (as opposed to, for example, earthquakes). This estimate considers only trends in climate-related disasters, but the results for all natural disasters would be virtually identical. By 2015, on average over 375 million people per year are likely to be affected by climate-related disasters. This is over 50% more than have been affected in an average year during the last decade. Between 1980 and 2007, EM-DAT contains records of over 6,500 climate-related natural hazard events, with an average of 343 events per year over the past decade (77% of all natural hazard events). The EM-DAT database not only gives counts of the numbers of disaster events over time, but also the total number of those affected by the event (Tables 1 and 2 below). The total number of people affected by an event includes those who suffered physical injuries or illness, as well as those made homeless or who otherwise required immediate assistance during a period of emergency. Between 1998 and 2007 in an average year, some 243 million people were affected by climate change related disasters.

TABLE 1
**Categories of Natural Hazard Disaster Types with Total Affected**

| *Natural Hazard Sub-Group* | *Natural Hazard Disaster Type* | *Total Affected, 1998-2007 (thousands)* |
|---|---|---|
| Biological | Epidemic | 6,046 |
| | Insect Infestation | — |
| Climatological | Drought | 739,747 |
| | Extreme Temperature | 6,139 |
| | Wildfire | 2,255 |
| Geophysical | Earthquake (seismic activity) | 42,163 |
| | Volcano | 1,405 |
| Hydrological | Flood | 1,288,688 |
| | Mass Movement (wet) | 1,741 |
| Meteorological | Storm | 3,89,368 |
| Total for All Natural Hazards | | 2.477,552 |
| Total for Climate Related | | 2,427,938 |
| Percentage (Climate Related) | | 98% |

*Source* : CRED EM-DAT Global Natural Disaster Occurrence and Impact, 1998-2007.

Climate change is predicted to have a range of serious consequences, some of which will have impact over the longer-term, like spread of disease and sea level rise, while some have immediately obvious impacts, such as intense rain and flooding. While recognising the importance of the other predicted consequences of climate change, this report focuses on this

TABLE 2
**People Affected by Natural Disaster, Forecast for 2015**

| | *Affected Annually (millions)* | *% Increase from Current Average* |
|---|---|---|
| Annual Average 1998-2007 | 243 m | |
| 2015 Regression Forecast | 375 m | |
| Difference | 132 m | 54% |
| Lower Estimate (95% CI) | 336 m | 38% |
| Upper Estimate (95% CI) | 413 m | 70% |

*Source* : CRED EM-DAT Global Natural Disaster Occurrence and Impact, 1980-2007.

second category: the 'extreme weather events' responsible for natural disasters. They include:

- Extreme temperature highs heat waves,
- Storms, including windstorms, hurricanes, etc.
- High levels of precipitation, and associated flooding, and
- Lack of precipitation, and associated drought.

Note that there are also important impacts from 'secondary' effects of climatic events e.g. avalanches, rock falls, landslides due to flooding, and forest fires in areas of drought.

Potential changes in climate-related extreme weather can be broken into three categories: in the first case there are more frequent or severe simple extremes (like higher temperatures), secondly, changes in complex extremes (like windstorms), which rely on a confluence of forces to come about, and third the possibility of major disastrous climate events such as the cessation of the thermohaline circulation which, though they would fundamentally change regional climates, are unlikely. An extreme event becomes a disaster when vulnerable areas are affected. Vulnerability can described by location and by issue:

- Any populated area exposed to a potential threat will by definition mean a higher potential for greater numbers of people being affected; moving population into areas likely to be affected is thus inviting trouble.
- Coastal zones, which are both exposed to storms and which harbour delicate ecosystems like wetlands.
- Flood plains/riversides, which are both exposed to flooding and often attractive for population and agriculture.
- Special, or already marginal habitats: alpine, arid, arctic, rainforest, etc., which depend on particular conditions for their unique character.

- Agriculture, fisheries and forestry are economic activities tied to nature and hence can be devastated by natural disasters
- Water resources are fundamental to human health and economic activity the interruption or pollution or drinking water, the lack of rainfall or irrigation for crops can put vulnerable populations in danger both in acute circumstances and over the long-term.

While more extreme events will over the course of time mean more potential disasters, it is possible to reduce the vulnerability of populations, areas and activities. This means that disasters are potentially avoidable, even given worsening climatic conditions.

## Natural Disaster

A natural disaster is a low probability high consequence event emanating from the nature that seriously affects the resources and socio-economic processes of the affected region. As per Anthony Oliver-Smith (1998): "A disaster is a process or event involving the combination of a potentially destructive agent from the natural, modified and/or constructed environment and population in a socially and economically produced condition of vulnerability, resulting in a perceived disruption of the customary relative satisfactions of individual and social needs for physical survival, social order and meaning.

Each year, more than 700 major natural disaster events shatter lives, destroy assets, and disrupt communities across broad geographic regions, particularly in developing countries. What impact do these natural disasters have on the development of poor countries? It is well known that natural disasters cause sharp increases in poverty; what is uncertain is the extent of their long-term impact on the economic viability of developing nations. The impact of natural disasters depends on two factors: the magnitude of the direct losses due to the event and the economic resilience of the country at the time the event strikes.

The plan of the present paper is as follows. The first section outlines different forms of natural disaster and their impacts along with identification of some proximate causes for these disasters. In section II, we discuss the link between natural disaster and economic growth and explain the trajectory of the growth paths that are affected by the sudden occurrence of natural disasters. Section III makes a survey of existing literature on theoretical models on natural disasters, while section IV discusses natural catastrophe modeling. In section V, we discuss the insurance against natural disaster as a strategy for its mitigation, while in section VI the various issues relating to managing the impact of natural disaster are discussed as revealed in some recent literature. The final section gives concluding observations.

## SECTION I
## FORMS OF NATURAL DISASTER

### 1. Important Forms of Natural Disasters

#### (a) Earthquakes

An earthquake is the rapid relative displacement of the rock on either side of a fracture, or fault, in the interior of the solid earth. The energy released by a sudden slip along a fault plane produces seismic waves that radiate outward in all directions from the initial point of rupture and that cause the ground to shake at the earth's surface. The area over which these seismic waves propagate is primarily a function of the amount of total energy released and the characteristics of the underlying rocks in the region. Certain regions of the earth's crust are geologically young and tend to attenuate, or dampen, wave propagation at a faster rate. California in the western part of the United States is such a region. In contrast, the New Madrid Seismic Zone (NMSZ) which extends from northwest Arkansas to southern Indiana in the central United States is geologically much older; the underlying rocks are harder and less fractured and can therefore propagate seismic waves over longer distances.

The distribution of global seismic activity is very well explained by the theory of plate tectonics. In broad terms, the theory describes the earth's lithosphere, which extends from the earth's surface down to a depth of approximately 80 kilometers, as consisting of several large and fairly stable slabs of relatively rigid rock called plates. Motion along the boundaries of these plates, can result in earthquakes of very large magnitude. Most of the earth's seismic energy is released along these plate boundaries. Other earthquakes are associated with crustal faults; still others, so-called intraplate earthquakes, occur within the interior of seemingly stable tectonic plates. Japan is located at the confluence of three tectonic plates (Pacific plate, Eurasian plate and Philippine plate) and is also characterized by a high density of surface faults. This unique setting makes Japan one of the most seismically active regions of the world. It must be emphasized that although earthquakes that occur on crustal faults contribute only to a small fraction of the total seismic energy released, they can potentially cause extremely high damage because they can be located closer to population centers e.g. 1994 Northridge earthquake in California. The NMSZ is a region of intraplate seismic activity. Typically, the recurrence rate of significant events in intraplate zones is relatively low.

#### (b) Tropical Cyclones

Tropical cyclones form where there is a convergence of the necessary conditions, which include a large expanse of warm ocean water (generally, water temperatures must be at least 80 degrees Fahrenheit) and the relative absence of "vertical shear", or winds that change appreciably in either magnitude or direction, thus "shearing-off" the cyclonic outflow at high altitudes. Tropical cyclones are most likely to form in the tropical regions of all of the earth's ocean basins, between about 5 degrees and 20 degrees latitude. The most active months are August and September in the Northern Hemisphere, and January and February in the Southern Hemisphere. The rising warm, dense air near the ocean's surface creates an area of low pressure, technically known as a depression. When wind speeds reach 40 miles per hour, the depression reaches tropical storm status. At wind speeds of 74 miles per hour, the storm is designated as a hurricane, or typhoon.

### (c) *Extratropical Cyclones*

Extratropical cyclones emerge out of interaction of cold and warm air masses in an unstable environment. Extratropical storm systems comprise of multiple areas of relatively low and high pressure, the locations of which can change quickly and frequently. In contrast, tropical storm systems in low latitudes exhibit symmetric structures. As an extratropical system evolves, the interaction of these low and high-pressure areas creates changes in the horizontal pressure gradient field. The windfield associated with such a system is driven in response to the evolving pressure gradient field. The mid-latitudes (between 35 and 60 degrees latitude) of both the Pacific, near the Asian coast, and the Atlantic, near Greenland and the North American coasts are the most favorable for extratropical cyclone formation. Storms affecting Europe typically originate to the east of North America or Greenland and subsequently move eastward across Europe. While cyclogenesis occurs every month of the year, formation into significant extratropical storms almost always occurs during the late fall, winter, or early spring. These systems are, therefore, often referred to simply as "winter storms". Extra-tropical cyclones typically do not achieve the intensity, in terms of wind speeds, that tropical cyclones achieve. However, a single extratropical cyclone can affect an area of tens of thousands of square miles and can subject individual locations to high winds for up to several days. In Europe, on average, 25 storms form each year of which five have the potential to cause substantial damage.

## 2. Natural Disasters—A Brief Overview

Since the 1970's, the two largest reinsurance companies in the world, Munich Re and Swiss Re, maintain comprehensive records on the frequency and severity of natural disasters. For the past decade, each firm has published comprehensive annual reports on the worldwide costs of natural disasters. As well, Munich Re has published reports examining trends over the past 10 and 25 years, as well as a map describing all natural disasters during the prior decade. Swiss Re also publishes reports on natural disasters on at least an annual basis, with additional reports issued on specific issues. While the measurement tools used by each firm are different, the basic conclusions of their studies are quite similar.

Windstorms, including hurricanes, and flooding each account for approximately 35 percent of the number of natural disasters and 30% of the annual damage caused by disasters. Earthquakes are responsible for 15% of the total number of events, and 30% of the total damage. The number of windstorms and flooding events have both increased in the past decade, while the number of earthquakes has remained relatively constant (Munich Re, 1998a). Despite the concentration of capital assets in the developed *versus* the developing world, the economic impacts of disasters are relatively evenly split between these groups of countries. While windstorms and flooding each account for approximately 30% of the annual average direct damage from disasters, their impacts on the developed and developing countries are significantly different. Windstorms are responsible for 70% of the private property damage from natural disasters in the United States (Swiss Re, 1999). Floods primarily occur in Asia, which bears 70% of worldwide flooding damage (Munich Re, 1998a). Earthquake damage during the past few decades has been more evenly split between the developed and the developing world. Consequently, the developed world primarily bears the costs of windstorm, the developing world the cost of flooding, and they divide the cost of earthquake damage. In the end, the developing world bears approximately USD 35 billion in direct costs of natural disasters, the same as the developed world. Based on the enormous disparity in the GDP for the two regions of the world, the per capita cost of natural disasters in relation to GDP in the developing world is dramatically higher. The damage variance between years is dramatic. During the past decade, the range has been between a high of USD 130 billion, and a low of 30 billion USD (Munich Re, 1998). In addition, the use of mean damage amounts may significantly discount the severity of events for limited geographical regions. For example, in 1998 the total worldwide economic losses are estimated to be approximately 65.5 billion USD (Swiss Re, 1999). Over half of those losses, 35 billion USD were Asian flooding losses, with 30 billion USD attributable to the losses in China from the immense flooding along the Yangtze River. The second largest single disaster was hurricane Mitch, with losses of 5 billion USD. As a result, 66% of 1998 losses were incurred by the developing world (Swiss Re, 1999).

During the last two decades, both the number and severity of natural disasters have been increasing. During the decade of the 1990's, the number of disasters has increased five times, and the damages have increased by nine times, contrasted to the decade of the 1960's (Munich Re, 1999). Between (1992-2001), losses arising out of natural disasters have remained about $ 65 billion a year.

During the decade of 1987-1997, the total direct economic loss from natural disasters was 700 billion USD, for an average loss of 70 billion USD. These increasing losses are attributable to both social factors, increasing concentration in hazard-prone urban regions, as well as larger and more frequent weather events The enormity of these losses has focused attention on how natural disasters undermine the developing countries' long term efforts to attain sustainable growth.

Three main categories of natural disasters account for 90% of the world's direct losses: floods, earthquakes, and tropical cyclones (hurricanes and typhoons, primarily). These three events periodically revisit the same geographic zones. Often, the losses can be significant portions of GDP. Swiss Re has identified a series of developing countries for whom losses from floods could be expected to exceed 1% of GDP. Among those countries are Argentina, Ecuador, Honduras, Nicaragua, and China. Brazil has potential losses that approach 1%. Munich Re identifies 28 developing countries that have suffered direct losses of more than 1 billion USD from natural disasters in the past 20 years. For small countries, losses much less than 1 billion USD can have significant long-term consequences.

## 3. Factors Responsible for Natural Disasters

### (a) Global Warming

Many scientists believe that global warming is responsible for the increasing frequency and severity of extreme weather events like floods, hurricanes, windstorms, and droughts and Asia and Latin America will bprobably feel the effects of climate change the most. The Inter-governmental Panel on Climate Change (IPPC) forecasts a 90 to 99 percent chance that, over the next 50 years, floods and droughts will become more common in Latin America, rising sea levels will threaten the survival of some island states, and tropical cyclones will become more intense.

### (b) Urbanization

The growing urbanization of the world's population has compounded the problem: even a minor event can cause significant damage in a heavily populated area. The proportion of people in developing countries who live in cities has doubled since 1960. More than 40 percent now live in urban areas, and this figure is expected to surpass 55 percent by 2030. Table 3 shows the projected growth in population in some of the megacities between 2000 and 2015.

Nearly 50% of the megacities of the world are subject to extreme weather events because of the same features that made them attractive to settlerssuch as natural flood plains, alluvial soil, and river or sea access. Fourteen of the world's 19 megacities with 10 million or more inhabitantsare in coastal zones, and over 70 of the world's 100 largest cities can expect a strong earthquake at least once every 50 years. Ninety-four percent of the world's major disasters in 1990-98 were in developing countries, according to the World Bank's World Development Report 2000-01. However, these countries have made fewer efforts than developed countries to adapt their physical environments to mitigate the impact of natural disasters or to insure themselves against disaster risk, partly because of the disincentive known as the "Samaritan's dilemma". The dilemma arises whenever those at risk (whether private sector parties or governments of vulnerable countries) expect to receive support if disaster strikes (from their national government or foreign donors) and therefore underinvest in protective measures—physical and financial to reduce the costs they will incur when it does strike. And, given the humanitarian imperative, it is hard for those in position to make a credible commitment to scale back post-disaster assistance even if those suffering did not take appropriate protective measures.

TABLE 3
**The Risky Megacities**

| *Cities with population> 10 million in 2000* | *Population (2000) (in million)* | *Projected Population (2015) (in million)* |
|---|---|---|
| Tokyo | 26.4 | 26.4 |
| Mexico City | 18.1 | 19.2 |
| Mumbai | 18.1 | 26.1 |
| Sau Paulo | 17.8 | 20.4 |
| Shanghai | 17.0 | 19.1 |
| New York | 16.6 | 17.4 |
| Lagos | 13.4 | 23.2 |
| Los Angeles | 13.1 | 14.1 |
| Kolkata | 12.9 | 17.3 |
| Karachi | 11.8 | 19.2 |
| New Delhi | 11.7 | 16.8 |
| Osaka | 11.0 | 11.0 |
| Manila | 10.9 | 14.8 |
| Beijing | 10.8 | 12.3 |
| Rio de Janeiro | 10.6 | 11.9 |
| Cairo | 10.6 | 13.8 |

*Source* : U.N. Population Division, March 2000.

## 4. The Natural Disaster Poverty Nexus

Twenty-four of the 49 poorest countries face a high level of disaster risk; as at least 6 of them have been hit by 28 major disasters in each of the past 15 years. The average frequency of disaster in the 77 poor countries eligible for support under the IMF's Poverty Reduction and Growth Facility (PRGF) is both high and apparently rising.

Small island states are also especially at risk because of their small economies, dependence on agriculture and tourism, and narrow resource base. Some may eventually disappear. Although economic losses stemming from natural disasters are smaller, in absolute terms, in developing than in developed countries, because of lower levels of infrastructure and capital stock, they are far higher relative to GDP.

Between 1985 and 1999, the world's wealthiest countries sustained 57.3 percent of the direct losses caused by disasters, representing 2.5 percent of their combined GDP; the world's poorest countries accounted for only 24.4 percent of losses, but their losses represented 13.4 percent of their combined GDP. Loss of life, moreover, is far greater in developing countries. More than 97 percent of all deaths from natural disasters in 1990-98 were in developing countries. Within developing countries, the poor are more likely to suffer than the rich because of the following reasons:

(i) First, they often live in areas especially vulnerable to destructive events such as floods, hurricanes, and landslides (not least because high-risk housing is more affordable).
(ii) Second, disasters can severely depress the food production of the rural poor.
(iii) Third, even small reductions in income can have a dramatic impact on the poor: their savings are unlikely to be adequate in the event of large-scale or multiple disasters, and they may be forced to sell real assets such as agricultural land and livestock.
(iv) Fourth, damage to water supply and transport infrastructures hurt the poor more than they hurt the rich.
(v) Finally, the poor are less likely to have access to risk-sharing mechanisms like insurance. Disasters can substantially increase measured poverty. It has been estimated that El Niño increased headcount poverty in affected areas in Ecuador by more than 10 percentage points, and about 50 percent of the increase in headcount poverty in the Philippines during the 1998 crisis has been attributed to El Niño.

A clear link of natural disasters to poverty is through infrastructure. The linkages can be described in at least three components: access to infrastructure is often a measure of poverty, infrastructure is a key component of economic growth, and the loss of infrastructure may have significant indirect and secondary costs that directly impact the poor. In fact, access to sanitation, electricity, and clean water, all supplied by infrastructure, are measures of poverty. As stated by the Bank, lack of access to infrastructure is a welfare issue. Further, access to infrastructure for the rural poor, primarily irrigation and transportation, increases income that enables the poor to manage risk The maintenance of infrastructure is essential to maintain economic growth, the primary linchpin in reducing poverty. As it does every ten years, the World Bank in 1990 discussed its role in reducing poverty. In its report, the Bank outlined the principles for its strategy in the 1990's for reducing poverty. As the Bank reported: Rapid and politically sustainable progress on poverty has been achieved by pursuing a strategy that has two equally important elements. The first element is to promote the productive use of the poor's most abundant asset-labor. The second is to provide basic social services to the poor. A comprehensive approach to poverty reduction, therefore, calls for a program of well-targeted transfers and safety nets as an essential complement to the basic strategy (World Bank, 1991). These principles have guided the Bank's lending activity. The report also specified particular characteristics of the poor that are also important to understand. These include the following:

(a) One-third of the total population of the developing world are poor and 18% of these are extremely poor;
(b) Nearly half of the developing world's poor, and half of those in extreme poverty, live in South Asia;
(c) Poverty is at its worst in rural areas; and
(d) Agricultural is still the main source of income for the world's poor. The livelihood of rural poor are linked to farming, whether or not they earn their income directly from it.

These facts lead to a strategy to reduce poverty that increases the income of rural poor through farming. Infrastructure development plays an essential role in reducing rural poverty. Infrastructure projects with a direct impact on rural agricultural production, primarily transportation, irrigation, and electricity, have a particularly direct impact on poverty reduction. In a study examining the role of infrastructure and agricultural production, the Bank reported that greater infrastructure development for agricultural development was associated with a one third increase in average household incomes, 24% increase in crop income, 92% increase in wage income, and income for livestock and fisheries increased by 78%. These changes associated with greater infrastructure development largely benefited the poor (World Bank, 1994). The Bank estimates that a one per cent increase in the stock of infrastructure translates to a one per cent increase in GDP. To reduce rural poverty, effective infrastructure projects related to agricultural have proven to be an essential policy tool. Natural disasters destroy essential rural infrastructure. In Asia, which accounts for half the number of the natural disasters in the world, and 70% of all floods, the average annual costs of floods over the past decade is approximately 15 billion USD (Munich Re, 1998). A high proportion of losses from flooding is to infrastructure. By some estimates, infrastructure loss accounts for 65% of all flood loss (Swiss Re, 1997). For Asia, this would account for average annual infrastructure loss of approximately 12 billion USD for the past decade. As more infrastructures is developed in rural areas to combat poverty, and as the frequency and severity of natural disasters also increase, the impacts on the poor will become more critical. The size of the loss to infrastructure can be compared to the worldwide lending activity of the World Bank. Over the past decade the Bank has annually loaned approximately 25 billion USD (Kreimer, 1998). The direct damage to infrastructure in Asia alone approximates nearly 50% of the total lending activity of the Bank. Rural infrastructure loss in the developing world has impacted the activity of the world's international lending institutions. The World Bank has estimated that it has loaned 14 billion USD to developing countries in the last 20 years for damages from natural disasters. This is nearly 2.5 times the amount loaned by the Bank for relief from civil disturbances worldwide (Kreimer, 1998). The Asian Development Bank has estimated that between 1988-98, 5.6% of ADF loans were for disaster rehabilitation. In 1992, nearly 20% of the ADF loans were for rehabilitative assistance from natural disasters (Arriens, 1999). The World Bank has internally estimated during the past decade that in Mexico up to 35% of its lending earmarked for infrastructure has been diverted to pay for the costs of Mexican natural disasters.The economic data generally available regarding the costs of natural disasters is primarily the direct economic costs. To date, not much work has been done to measure the indirect impacts of natural disasters to developing countries. While measuring indirect impacts is much more difficult than measuring direct property loss, the implications of the indirect costs can be much more severe. Some studies measuring the impacts of the loss of flows from infrastructure indicate that damage may be 2.5 times the cost of the direct losses (Shinozuka, 1998). The current state of the art tends to measure the direct economic loss caused by natural disasters. In fact, almost all the data referenced in this paper is based on these data sources. This tendency tends to distort policy decision making as relates to disasters. For example, these types of analysis focus attention on disasters as single events. For most countries harmed by disasters, they are repeated events that may strike at random times but impact both the rate and pattern of development (Arriens, 1999). Without considering natural disasters as patterns of events with indirect and secondary effects, the costs of the events tend to be minimized. As such, policy options such as mitigation and risk transfer do not receive their proper due as tools to reduce the long-range cost of natural disasters.

## 5. Macroeconomic Impact of Natural Disaster

The destruction of physical assets, including capital stock, infrastructure, natural resources, and, not least, labor, has both a short- and a long-term impact on macroeconomic performance in some countries, while natural disasters have caused only minor economic disruptions in others. In 25 country-specific studies, the United Nations Economic Commission for Latin America and the Caribbean (ECLAC) found that the worse socioeconomic conditions were at the time a disaster struck, the stronger its impact. In the wake of a natural disaster, a country's tax base shrinks while its spending needs rise. Because disasters are small relative to their economies, developed countries have the flexibility to meet the cost of disaster relief by some mix of temporary tax increases. Germany temporarily raised taxes, for instance, after the 2002 floodsand borrowing. It is far more difficult for developing countries to raise taxes. Unless they receive external grants, they must either increase borrowing or resort to monetization. Along with the deterioration of their fiscal position, affected countries may suffer a weakening of their trade balance, as declining production of export goods and post-disaster reconstruction boost demand for imports and divert tradables to the home market. These developments, combined with the flight of panicky foreign investors, put downward pressure on the exchange rate, resulting in inflationary pressures. Disasters depress not only the immediate macroeconomic outlook but also the balance sheet positions of key economic sectors. Public sector debt ratios are likely to worsen and domestic saving. to decline, forcing both the private and the public sectors to increase their borrowing abroad.

## SECTION II

# NATURAL DISASTER AND ECONOMIC GROWTH

### Introduction

Catastrophic disasters create significant and intense damages to the capital stocks, and sometimes to the labor (for example, more than 6,000 casualties in the Kobe earthquake, 1995). While these damages are serious and extensive, the effects of these damages to the long-term economic growth of a developed county are still limited (Okuyama Hewings and Sonis, 1999). However, these damages become quite serious in the context of regions and of developing countries. In this section, the effects of a disaster in growth theory context is analyzed and discussed, in order to offer some insights for the effects of a disaster to the transition of long-term growth. The analysis is based on Okuyama (2003).

For simplification, a basic Neo-Classical model of the Solow-Swan model (Solow, 1956; and Swan, 1956) is employed in this paper. Let us consider, for a moment, if technological progress can be neglected, the production function of an economy can be set as:

$$Y = F\ (K, L) \tag{1}$$

where $Y$ is the total output, $K$ is the level of capital accumulation, and $L$ is the level of labor population. The use of per capita term for output and capital makes Equation (8) the intensive form:

$$y = f(k) \tag{2}$$

where $y = Y/L$, and $k = K/L$. Set that saving rate (constant) is $s$, capital depreciation is $\delta$ (constant), and population growth rate is $n$ (constant). The change in per capita capital stock over time becomes as follows:

$$k = s.f(k)-(n+\delta).k$$

where $k = dk/dt$. Thus, the steady state level of capital accumulation, $k^*$ where $k^* = 0$, satisfies the following condition:

$$s.f(k^*) = (n+\delta).k^*$$

This steady state condition can be seen as the point A in diagram 1. Now, suppose that an economy is at the steady state 3 and that a catastrophic disaster occurred and the capital stocks were severely damaged, but no casualties in labor population; thus the per capita capital level went down to the decreased level, $k_a$, where $k_a < k^*$.

This economy's output decreased, due to the damages from a disaster, from the steady state level, $v^*$, to the damaged level, $y_d$. Because of the damages and the decreased level of per capita capital stock, the economy is now out of its steady state, and has some space (the distance between points **B** and **C**) for the growth (recovery) of per capita capital accumulation. Therefore, the economy picks up a speed to increase the level of per capita capital from $k_d$ toward $k^*$, as the recovery process. At the same time, during the recovery period, resources (output) are allocated more toward the reconstruction of damaged capital stocks than under the normal circumstances without a disaster. This implies that the saving rate for the capital accumulation may become higher than the previous level, $s$. This recovery saving rate is set as $s_r$ (where $s_r > s$ ), may accelerate the speed of recovery, capital reaccumulation, further (the distance between **D** and **C**, which is much wider than between **B** and **C**), as shown in diagram 1. However, as the economy recovers, the recovery saving rate should gradually go back to the normal rate, $s$, and as the level of capital accumulation becomes close to the steady state level, (**D** to **A** in Figure 1), the speed of recovery is close to zero.

The transitional dynamics of recovery can be further illustrated by the use of the growth rate of $k$. The growth rate of $k$, $y$ $k$, can be given based on Equation.

$$\gamma_k = k/k = s.f(k)/k-(n-\delta) \quad (3)$$

Diagram 2 indicates the transitional dynamics around the steady state of the Solow-Swan model.

At the steady state, $k^*$, the growth rate becomes zero due to the intersection of two lines,

$$s.f(k)/k = (n+\delta)$$

FIG. 1

**Solow-Swan Model and a Disaster Situation**

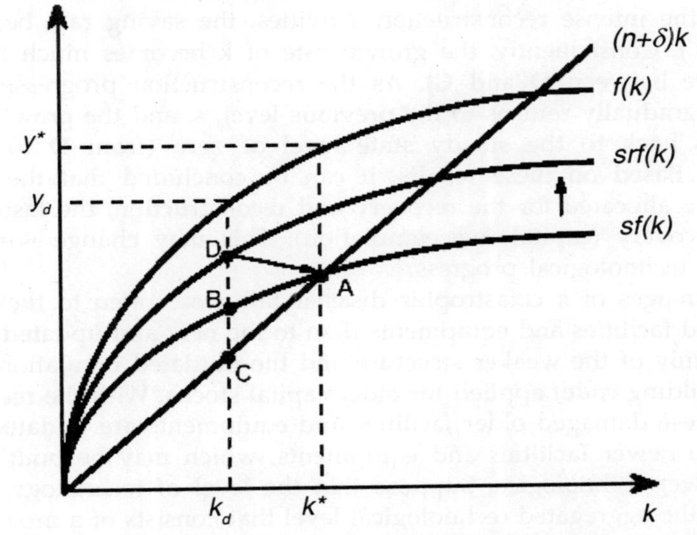


*Source* : Y. Okuyama (2003): "Economics of Natural Disasters: A Critical Review", Paper presented at the 50th North American Meeting, Regional Science Association International, November 20-22, 2003, Philadelphia, PA.

FIG. 2

**The Transitional Dynamics of Recovery**

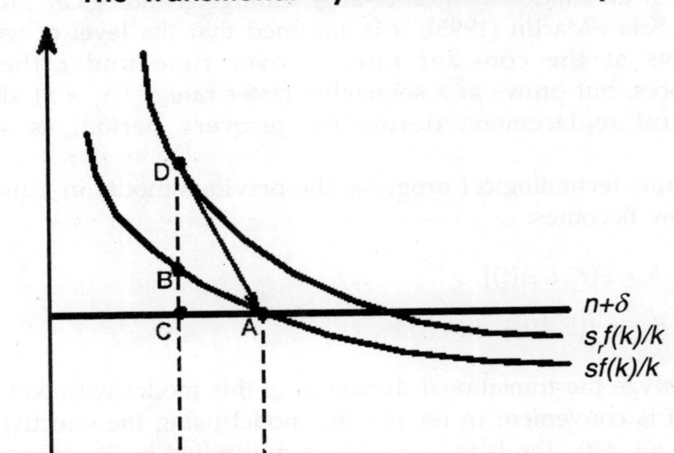


*Source* : Y. Okuyama (2003): "Economics of Natural Disasters: A Critical Review", Paper presented at the 50th North American Meeting, Regional Science Association International, November 20-22, 2003, Philadelphia, PA.

With a natural disaster, the level of per capita capital becomes $k_d$, and due to this departure from the steady state, the growth rate of *k* becomes positive (the distance between **B** and **C** in Figure 3). As in the above, because of the intense reconstruction activities, the saving rate becomes higher (to $s_r$). Consequently, the growth rate of k becomes much higher (the distance between **D** and **C**). As the reconstruction progresses, the saving rate gradually returns to the previous level, s, and the growth rate of *k* moves back to the steady state level of zero (from **D** to **A** in diagram 2). Based on these results, it can be concluded that the more resources are allocated for the recovery and reconstruction, the faster the speed of recovery (capital re-accumulation). This may change with the inclusion of technological progress.

The damages of a catastrophic disaster fall more often to the older and outdated facilities and equipments than to the new and updated ones, because mainly of the weaker structure and the outdated regulations (for instance, building code) applied for older capital stocks. With the recovery activities, these damaged older facilities and equipments are updated and upgraded to newer facilities and equipments, which may be built upon and use newer technologies. Suppose that the level of technology in an economy is the aggregated technological level that consists of a mixture of old and new capital stocks, and that the recovery activities increase the rate of technological progress to some extent by updating the technological level of damaged older capital (Figure 2). This increase of the rate of technological progress is strictly temporary, since the recovery activities cannot progress the level of technology *per se*. Following the example of the Solow-Swan model with labor-augmenting technological progress by Barro and Sala-i-Martin (1995), it is assumed that the level of technology, *A(t)*, grows at the constant rate, *x*, over time under the normal circumstances, but grows at a somewhat faster rate, $x_r$ ($x_r > x$), due to the technological replacement, during the recovery period, as shown in Figure 3.

With this technological progress, the previous model in Equations (1) and (3) now becomes:

$$Y = F[K, L.A(t)] \tag{4}$$

$$\dot{k} = s.f[k.A(t)] - (n+\delta).k \tag{5}$$

To analyze the transitional dynamics of this model with technological progress, it is convenient to rewrite the model using the effective amount of labor, $\dot{L} \equiv L.A(t)$, the labor population multiplied by its efficiency, *A(t)*. Then, the quantity of capital per unit of effective labor, $\dot{k}$ can be defined as:

$$\dot{k} = K/\dot{L} = K/[L.A(t)] = k/A(t) \tag{6}$$

FIG. 3

**Technological Progress and a Disaster**

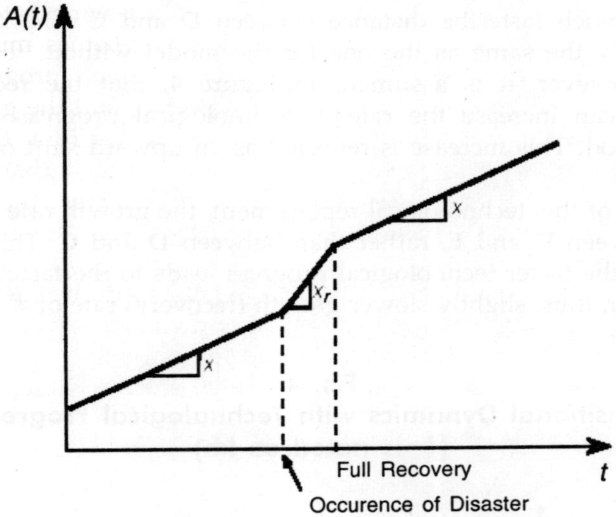


*Source* : Y. Okuyama (2003): "Economics of Natural Disasters: A Critical Review", Paper presented at the 50th North American Meeting, Regional Science Association International, November 20-22, 2003, Philadelphia, PA.

With the quantity of output per unit of effective labor, $\dot{y} = Y/L$ the intensive form of the model becomes:

$$\dot{y} = f(\dot{k}) \tag{7}$$

Hence, Equation (5) now becomes:

$$\dot{k} = s.f(\dot{k}) - (x+n+\delta).\dot{k} \tag{8}$$

Also, the growth rate of $\dot{k}$ is:

$$\gamma_k = s.f(\dot{k})/k - (x+n+\delta) \tag{9}$$

At the steady state, $\dot{k}$ becomes $\dot{k}^*$ since its growth rate becomes zero (diagram 3)

$$s.f(\dot{k}^*)/\dot{k}^* = (x+n+\delta) \tag{10}$$

The economy suffers from a natural disaster, and a part of capital stocks are damaged and destroyed; thus, the quantity of capital per unit of effective labour becomes from the steady state level, $\dot{k}^*$, to the damaged level, $k_d$. At this point, the growth rate of recovery is the distance between

**B** and **C**, if no special allocation of resources to recovery is made. For the faster recovery, the saving rate can be increased to allocate more resources to capital re-accumulation; thus, as in the previous case, the growth rate of $\dot{k}$ becomes much fasterthe distance between **D** and **C**. The story up to now is exactly the same as the one for the model without technological progress. However, it is assumed, in Figure 4, that the technological replacement can increase the rate of technological progress during the recovery period. This increase is reflected as an upward shift of $x + n + \delta$ to $x_r + n + \delta$.

Because of this technological replacement, the growth rate of $\dot{k}$ is the distance between **D** and **E**, rather than between **D** and **C**. This is due to the fact that the faster technological progress leads to the faster growth of effective labor, thus, slightly slower growth (recovery) rate of $\dot{k}$ than in the previous case.

FIG. 4

**Transitional Dynamics with Technological Progress ($\dot{k}$ is noted as kh)**

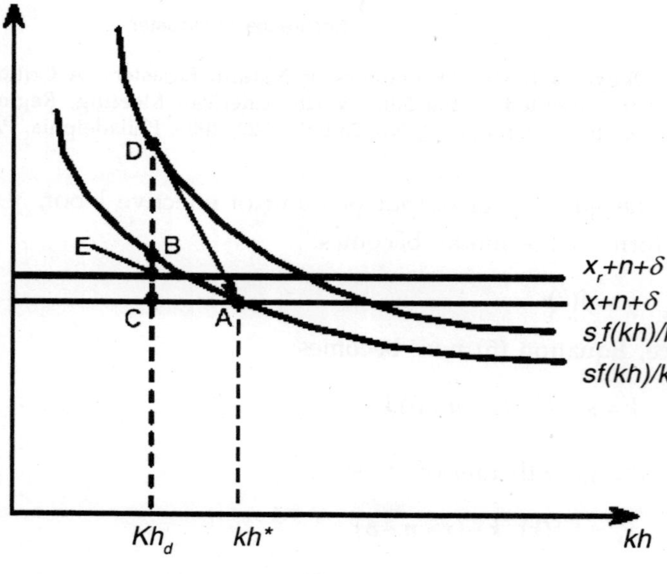


*Source* : Y. Okuyama (2003): "Economics of Natural Disasters: A Critical Review", Paper presented at the 50th North American Meeting, Regional Science Association International, November 20-22, 2003, Philadelphia, PA.

These analyses guide toward two policy implications. First, the rate of recovery depends on the resource allocation to the recovery activities, i.e. increase of saving rate. However, the increase in saving rate implies the decline in consumption level. In this context, the analysis could be extended to employ the Ramsey model analysis with consumer optimization (Ramsey, 1928; Cass, 1965; and Koopmans, 1965). In this way, the optimum allocation of resources for recovery in the growth context can be studied. Secondly, the degree of mixture between old and new capital stocks in an economy can influence the recovery rate of $\dot{k}$. This implies that the technological progress during the normal circumstances become more important. For this type of investigation, the model needs to be stretched to employ the framework of endogenous growth models to compare different policies of technological progress and the impacts on disaster recovery.

The theoretical discussion and analysis of disaster is important to augment our knowledge for the impacts and consequences of a disaster, and our preparedness against them. While disasters are not frequently repeated phenomena and the damages from a disaster vary considerably from one disaster to another (even in the same type of disaster, such as earthquake) and from one region to another, this type of generalized analysis of theory can assist empirical analysis of disasters in a number of ways. For example, the effects of uncertainty after a disaster need to be incorporated in the analysis of economic impacts of the disaster, since the decision-making and response to supply and/or demand changes can be noticeably different from the ones in the pre-disaster context. The usual assumptions of laws of supply and demand laid in the conversional models, such as Computable General Equilibrium (CGE) models, need to take into account this uncertainty and behavioral changes. Furthermore, uncertainty may create sizeable influence to the production planning, especially for manufacturing sectors which decide the level of production with the anticipation of future demand stream, and may bring additional impacts on inventory management and production scheduling. In addition, the theoretical analysis of disaster impacts may offer some new perspectives to the disaster related research. For example, we have discussed above the issues of technological replacement and optimal saving rate, in the context of long-term growth of the economy experiencing natural disasters. As in the endogenous growth theory, in the long-run, technological progress becomes the driving force of economic growth. While technological replacement or update resulted from the reconstruction of damaged capital stocks by a disaster is different from usual technological progress in terms of its exogenous nature of shock, it is similar about the endogenous level of technology available for replacement. On the other hand, the speed of recovery depends on the extra amount of savings allocated to reconstruction activities. The result can be extended to examine the consequence of disaster insurance incorporating the consumption-saving optimization analysis for the study of long-run implications.

## SECTION III

## THEORETICAL AND EMPIRICAL MODELS ON NATURAL DISASTERS : A SURVEY OF LITERATURE

The economic problems produced by natural disasters have long occupied the attention of mankind. Along with preparation for war and self defense, the response to problems of flood, drought, earthquake, and windstorms has been used as a test of the ability of governments and economic institutions to serve a population. In our own time, there is increasing concern with the unwillingness of private insurers to operate in high risk areas and with the escalating cost of government disaster assistance. In spite of all this rationale for studying of the economics of natural disasters, a search of on-line sources for books, articles, and other academic publications on the subject provides only a modest number of references. Apparently, governments have found little need to examine the economic effects of their policies towards actual or potential natural disasters.

Although the literature is thin, it includes a surprising diversity of theoretical models and empirical results responding to a number of different issues and problems. Unfortunately, these individual approaches to the economics of natural disasters often bear little relation to one another because they proceed from very different assumptions and analyze different aspects of the relation between disasters and the economy. The first task of this review is to organize these approaches under a modest list of headings and to show the relations among them. Ideally, they would all be placed within the context of an overarching general statement of the economics of natural disasters but this review will settle for the more modest goal of identifying distinctive approaches and pointing out differences in their assumptions and purposes.

The information about the extent and level of damages from a disaster are critical, especially for the resource allocation in emergency response period. Obtaining such information may be costly and limited, or the obtained information can be incorrect and/or fabricated due to the chaotic nature of aftermath in a disaster. These informational asymmetry and the uncertainty may create further disturbances in economic activities and decision makings. In the mainstream economics, risk and uncertainty have been discussed since the Frank H. Knight's (1921) seminal work where he defined risk as referring to situations where the decision-maker can assign mathematical (objective) probabilities to the randomness which s/he is faced with, whereas 'uncertainty' refers to situations when this randomness cannot be expressed in terms of specific mathematical probabilities. Shackle (1979) and Davidson (1991), have argued that Knight's distinction is so critical that Knightian uncertainty may be the only relevant form of randomness for economics, in particular, when it is tied up with the issue of time and information, while Knightian risk is only possible in very controlled scenarios with very clear alternatives, such as gambling. In the disaster literature, risk and uncertainty are employed without any significant debate of their definitions. Dacy and Kunreuther used 'uncertainty' for the decision making analysis during emergency response period, describes in the sub-section of Problem of Information and Communication. However, based on the Knightian distinction, their model is clearly a risk model with objective probability for item usage, or perhaps, it might be somewhat connected to Savage's 'expected utility with subjective probabilities'. In the disaster studies many employed also the probabilistic occurrence of a disaster as 'risk' in order to derive the expected utility for decision-makings against disasters (for example, Howe and Cochrane, 1976; Brookshire, *et al.*, 1985; Boisvert, 1992; and Kunreuther and Roth, 1998). In these studies, more attention are directed toward pre-disaster analysis, such as risk management and disaster insurance, rather than toward the uncertainty created after a disaster.In the disaster-related research, it can be assumed that 'risk' refers to the occurrence of disasters or damages where decision-makers can assign mathematical probabilities for the randomness in a pre-disaster context whereas 'uncertainty' refers to the situations in the aftermath of a disaster where the situations and consequences cannot be expressed in terms of specific mathematical probabilities in a post-disaster context. In this way, 'risk' used in most studies, including the above, can retain its definition and can also have the solid distinction with 'uncertainty'. A major difference from the Knightian definition of 'uncertainty' is that the degree and extent of 'uncertainty' after a disaster is not fixed as emergency response and recovery starts, more information regarding the damages and recovery plan will become available; thus, the degree and extent of 'uncertainty' may diminish (see Figure 1). In a normal period before a disaster, some, but not significant, level of uncertainty may exist, such as business cycle and momentary fluctuations; at the time of disaster, the degree of uncertainty jumps up to a very high level, due to no information available about the extent of the damages on capital stocks and labor. This high level of uncertainty may continue in a short period, due to the continued lack of information and also to the confusion and depression under a chaotic situation created by the disaster. The length of this period depends on the size of the disaster and the extent of the damages. After this period, the information regarding the level and extent of damages become available; thus, the level of uncertainty may start declining. However, the speed of this decline can be influenced by many factors, such as the release timing of recovery plan, the priority of recovery, the damages to the other regions, etc. These uncertainties are difficult to be quantified with objective mathematical probabilities, and are also difficult to be measured even with the subjective-preference. Figure 5 on next page summarises the picture.

Fig. 5

**Degree of Uncertainty in and after a Disaster**

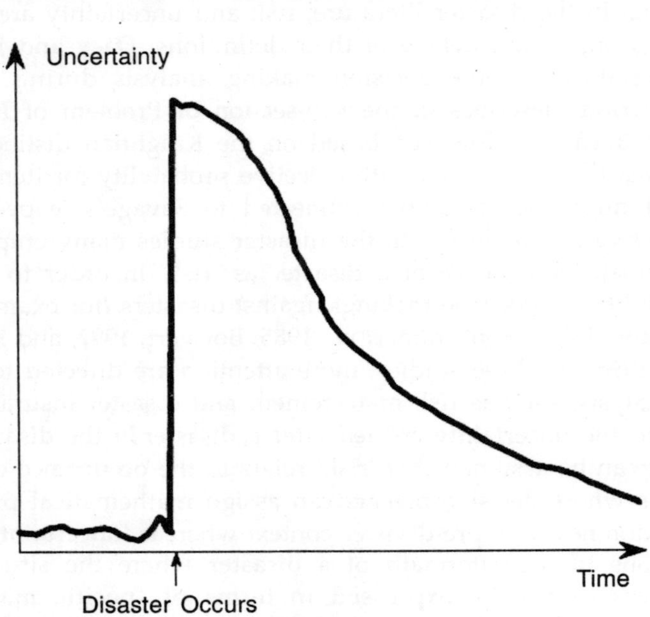


This uncertainty after a disaster can create some serious impacts to economic activities in terms of production planning (Okuyama *et al.*, 2004). However, in order to evaluate the economic impacts of a disaster, it is important to include the effects of this uncertainty, since uncertainty may create further disturbances and influences to decision-making for economic activities and recovery than most impact studies without it derived. Furthermore, during this uncertain period, other behavioural factors that are not common

without a disaster, such as sympathy and post-disaster cooperation and changes in consumption behaviour (Okuyama *et al.*, 1999), need to be considered to evaluate the full spectrum of impacts and the recovery process and path after a disaster.

## The Informational Effects of Natural Disasters

There is substantial evidence that natural disaster events have informational effects whether they occur or not and that the economic consequences of these *ex ante* effects may be larger than either the direct or indirect effects. Informational effects arise *ex ante* because disaster events are inherently local in character and expectations for future events, both their frequency and severity, are very disaster events over a period of time allows for substantial updating of these expectations. Surveys of households before and after disaster events show a substantial change in attitudes toward purchase of insurance and expenditures for mitigation. Brown (1972) provides an early discussion of the likely informational effects of disaster events and models a process in which prior expectations of disaster probabilities are subject to Bayesian updating based on recent disaster experience. Note that, in such models, non-occurrence is just as important as occurrence in its effect on expectations. Recent experience is added to the individual's information set and expectations are updated periodically.

The potential importance of disaster expectations was demonstrated by Ellison, Milliman, and Roberts (1984) through the use of a small region econometric model of the Charleston, South Carolina area that included investment equations in which expectations played a role. They were then able to simulate the effects of an earthquake under alternative *ex ante* informational scenarios: a fully anticipated event, an unanticipated earthquake, and an earthquake announcement with no subsequent earthquake. There are a number of features of this modeling effort that are noteworthy and will be discussed later but the essential informational feature is the comparison of an unanticipated event with a true prediction and a false prediction. Because the model was structured so that migration of labour and capital (investment) depended on expectations, credible earthquake predictions that are not believed have a substantial negative effect on output in the affected area. These negative effects would probably have been larger if the model had incorporated an option to invest in mitigation efforts. Ellison, Milliman, and Roberts (1984) reach conclusions that should be sobering for those who predict disasters. While they find that the present discounted value of local production when a local earthquake is correctly predicted is greater than the present discounted value of production when there is an unanticipated earthquake scenario, this gain from correct production of an earthquake occurrence is far less than the fall in present discounted value of production when an earthquake event is incorrectly forecast. The losses from an incorrect prediction exceed the gains from a correct prediction. If false announcements can have substantial *ex ante* information effects, then it follows that disaster events themselves may have information effects because they influence future expectations. This view is advanced in Brown (1972) and tested empirically in Yezer and Rubin (1987). Papers by MacDonald, Murdoch and White (1987), Shilling, Benjamin, and Sirmans (1985), and Brookshire, Thayer, Tschirhart, and Schulze (1985) relate the asset prices of housing in a given area to proximity to natural disaster hazards, flood planes or earthquake faults. The standard finding is that houses further from the hazard sell for higher prices that appear to reflect differences in insurance costs. Bernknopf, Brookshire, and Thayer (1990) demonstrate that the announcement of a probable future disaster in Mammoth, California had significant negative effects on both real property investment and residenial property values but not on recreational visitation. These results suggest that there is a market response, at least on the part of investors, to new information on disaster probabilities in a specific area. One limitation of these studies is that they involve comparisons of a single change in disaster probabilities. While this is sufficient to show the importance of information effects of natural disasters, it gives little insight into the dynamic component of expectations formation. It would be useful to know more about the process that individuals use to formulate their disaster expectations.

## Informational Effects of Disasters : Empirical Evidence

In addition to the Bernknopf, Brookshire, and Thayer (1990) demonstration of specific announcement effects in Mammoth, California, Rubin and Yezer (1987) tested a model in which the divergence between actual disasters and disaster expectations was related to changes in a local economy. First, they developed measures of the expected frequency of natural disasters for cities based on their previous disaster history. Comparison of this expected frequency, based on historical disaster rates, with subsequent disaster experience over a subsequent four-year period allowed them to compute the unanticipated component of recent disaster rates, based on the divergence between actual and expected (historical) disaster rates. Second, they identified the rate of change in the price of housing services as one appropriate indicator of the local economic effects of disaster expectations. Third, they estimated a model relating the number of disaster events, the number of unanticipated disaster events, and other factors to the change in local housing prices. The test results were consistent with expectations that the number of disaster events had no significant relation to house price changes but the unanticipated component of recent disaster experience was negatively related to the rate of house price appreciation. Specifically, occurrence of one unanticipated disaster event was estimated to lower house prices by 2%, or a negative effect of several hundreds of millions of dollars in a city with 250,000 households.

## Theoretical Effects of Disaster Expectations on Development

It is useful to compare models that include the information effects of unanticipated disasters with the results of models that ignore information effects and implicitly ignore local differences in disaster expectations. The evidence from case studies of disaster events is mixed. Many have shown significant long-term effects, both positive and negative. The record also contains observations of little or no effect. There are a few studies which indicate that natural disaster concerns are not particularly important among public officials, many of whom might be charged with dealing with their consequences. A major econometric study of a large national cross-section of disaster events occurring during the 1960-70 period, found no long term effects on population or housing trends. While this study might be criticized for using only population and housing units as indicators, the Rubin and Yezer (1987) results suggest that no significant effects would be observed even if housing or land price changes were being analyzed. Failure to find significant economic effects of the rate of occurrence of disaster events merely indicates that, on average, disaster events occur where they are expected. It does not imply that unanticipated increases in the frequency or severity of disaster events could not have significant economic consequences or attract the attention of public officials.

Models of natural disasters with information effects have significant implications for patterns of residential land use. These implications have been developed by Frame (1998) applying the standard (monocentric) urban model to a city with differentiated levels of natural disaster expectations. This application of the urban land market models has much in common with earlier modeling efforts by Scawthorn, Iemura, and Yamada (1982). Frame (1998) models a closed urban area in which a fixed number of households, earning a given market wage at a central location, choose housing quantity and location to maximize utility from consumption of housing and a composite good whose price does not vary. Within the urban area there are different location-specific expectations of the probability of damage from natural disasters. Because households are free to move throughout the city, the price of housing services must fall in less attractive area—i.e. areas with larger commuting cost to center city jobs or higher expectations of disasters. This is not a particularly strong assumption, given that it has been demonstrated in empirical studies by MacDonald, Murdoch and White (1987), Shilling, Benjamin, and Sirmans (1985), and Brookshire, Thayer, Tschirhart, and Schulze (1985). All of these studies have demonstrated the presence of price discounts for increases in expected risk, but empirical evidence on other market reactions, such as lower rates or investment or lower population densities have not been the object of substantial testing. Based on this assumption of household mobility, Frame (1998) is able to establish the following theoretical propositions regarding the effects of increasing the expected frequency of hazard events.

Producers of housing respond to the lower price per unit of housing services in areas with greater hazard risk by bidding less for undeveloped land in such areas and producing housing services with a lower ratio of capital to land—i.e. the ratio of housing services per unit land is lower in areas with greater hazard risk. In areas characterized by a mixture of high commuting cost and/or high hazard risk, land prices may be depressed to the point where no housing is built. The effect of the lower supply price of housing on quantity of housing demanded in areas with greater hazard risk is ambiguous because lower price encourages consumption and decreases the significance of any damage that is done but greater hazard risk also makes housing consumption less certain. Because the effect of greater hazard risk on quantity of housing demanded by households is ambiguous, it is also not possible to prove increasing risk lowers the density of opulation. However, this effect seems likely and certainly is true when increasing risk lowers developed land rents below the level needed to promote any residential development—i.e. when land is withheld from residential use, population density falls to zero. The model developed by Frame (1998), like the earlier efforts of Scawthorn, Iemura, and Yamada (1982), generates downward shifts of housing prices and development densities in parts of the urban area where disaster probability is high. This result fits intuition well, with natural hazards operating in a manner similar to any natural barrier that raises costs of producing housing. It is likely that analogous results could be obtained for noxious plants producing outputs on such sites although an additional consideration would involve any supplemental wage compensation required to attract workers to a hazardous site. Frame (1998) also provides a number of results on the effects of disaster insurance. Provision of unsubsidized insurance, at a price reflecting the actuarial value of future losses, allows households to diversify away geographic risk. Because the premium payment increases with expected loss, provision of unsubsidized insurance does not change the negative relation between hazard probability and the price of housing, and the density of housing production per unit land. If insurance is subsidized, the effect of hazard risk on housing prices and on the density of housing supplied is attenuated compared to the unsubsidized or no insurance cases. The positive effect of insurance subsidies on housing prices was noted empirically by Shilling, Sirmans, and Benjamin (1989). While these predicted effects of providing actuarially fair or subsidized insurance may generally agree with intuition, a final result provided by Frame (1998) is likely surprising. The effect of insurance, even subsidized insurance, on the density or welfare of population in high risk areas is ambiguous. It would be interesting to extend these results to open city models in which one city is subject to greater natural hazard risk and must compete for capital and labour against another city.

The Frame results are compatible with models of information updating in which recent rates of disaster activity or announcements of new disaster forecasts are used to update disaster expectations. This implies that either the recent rate of disaster events or announcements concerning such events can have information effects to the extent that expectations of future disaster events in that area are changed. The result will be a change in the prices of housing and land, and in desired density of development. These predictions appear to be testable.

## Models of the Insurance Market, Mitigation, and Post-Disaster Aid

The rising cost of insurance claims, both private and government sponsored, in the last decade has stimulated substantial interest in various aspects of the provision of insurance against losses from natural disasters. Among the most important issues appear to be:

(1) reluctance of individuals to purchase insurance and invest in mitigation efforts,

(2) the interaction among insurance, mitigation expenditures, and post-disaster aid and their effect on economic development, and
(3) the design of financial instruments appropriate for capitalizing private insurance against major disaster events.

Examples of the literature on these topics will be considered in turn. All three have been the object of significant recent research efforts motivated in no small part by the rising costs to both private insurance companies and government of natural disaster events in the United States during the 1990's.

## Behaviour and Perceptions of Property Owners in High Risk Areas

Significant efforts have been made assess if individuals in high risk areas perceive those risks and act upon them in their insurance and mitigation decisions. The National Flood Insurance Program (NFIP) has served as a poster child for non-participation. Kunreuther (1978) noted that, in the first four years on the program (1968-72), only 3,000 of 21,000 eligible communities with substantial flooding history participated in the program and fewer than 300,000 homeowners voluntarily purchased a policy. In spite of the fact that NFIP was subsidized, participation was only accelerated by threatening communities with denial of federally assisted or guaranteed post-disaster aid, specifically construction or mortgage loans, to property owners in non-participating communities that had been identified as special flood hazard areas. Palm, *et al.* (1990) have documented the failure of homeowners and even mortgage lenders to seek earthquake insurance in high risk areas.

Taken at face value, this stylized fact regarding failure to insure has, in the view of some, called into question the use of standard models of the economics of insurance in the special case of natural disasters. Kunreuther and Kleffner (1992) and Kunreuther (1996) have argued that homeowners do not behave as if they were maximizing expected utility in their decisions to purchase insurance or engage in private mitigation efforts. They hold that behaviour most closely resembles the contingent weighting model in which individuals place different weights on the probability of a hazard event and on the contingent loss should it occur. If individuals place low weights on the probability of infrequent natural hazard events, they will act as if the expected utility of insurance and mitigation is lower than that perceived by experts. The failure of the public to use seat belt restraints has been rationalized this way. Kunreuther and Kleffner (1992) consider simple benefit cost estimates of a loss mitigation measure, bracing pre-1940 homes in California so that they would not slide off their foundations. They find that low rates of mitigation appear to suggest low probabilities of hazard events—or low weighting of those probabilities. Overall, it appears that property owners in areas subject to natural hazard risk underspend on insurance and mitigation efforts compared to standards that are justified by sound benefit-cost analysis. Even where building codes require cost-effective mitigation efforts, Kunreuther (1996) reports serious cases of underinvestment and failure to comply, resulting in significant additional damage, for example, in the case of hurricane Andrew. In contrast to the evidence that property owners in high risk areas ignore those risks, research also indicates that their behaviour changes with additional information. While property owners are observed to be "insensitive" to levels of risk, they do respond to "changes" in risk. Most dramatic is the finding by Palm, *et al.* (1990) that, prior to the Loma Prieta earthquake, there was no relation between proximity to the San Andreas fault and the rate of purchase of earthquake insurance but that after the earthquake the purchase of insurance increased and that insurance rates fell with distance from the fault. Survey evidence indicates further that attitudes toward the importance of earthquake insurance shifted substantially after the Loma Prieta earthquake. There is also evidence that market prices reflect learning behaviour. Brookshire, Thayer, Tschirhart, and Schulze (1985) find that publication of information on the distance from properties and established fault lines causes house prices to fall within the earthquake prone zone. Shilling, Benjamin, and Sirmans (1985) found that NFIP subsidies to pre-FIRM structures were capitalized into house values. As noted in some detail above, Yezer and Rubin (1987) find that housing prices respond to unanticipated disaster events, i.e. to differences between the frequency of floods, windstorms, etc. during a given period and the previous history of such events. Thus it appears that the standard insurance model, in which expected loss and the variance in expected loss motivate behaviour, works in a dynamic context. Changes in disaster events have the predicted effect on property owners perceptions and behaviour as well as on market prices.

Research on the economic behaviours and responses of property owners in high hazard risk areas are, at least, partly consistent with standard expected utility models employed to explain expenditures for insurance and mitigation. Surely, more research is needed to resolve these issues and they are important to public policy toward insurance, mitigation, and post-disaster aid. One possible explanation for the failure of property owners in high risk areas to make insurance and mitigation decisions that appear economically justified is that they are selected into high hazard areas based on their perceptions of risks. If markets provide price discounts for properties in areas with greater hazard risk, those properties will be differentially attractive to individuals who fail to perceive the risks. Alternatively, if there is a risk distribution, those whose expectation of actual risk is at the low end of expert opinion will likely occupy properties in areas rated as highest risk by the experts. With low probability events where expert opinion on frequency has high variance, particularly events such as earthquakes, it would not be surprising if property owners in the highest risk areas believed that risks were at the low end of the distribution of expert opinion. Subsequent occurrence of an event, could have a dramatic effect on these expectations as survey evidence and behaviour have shown.

## Interaction Among Insurance, Development, Mitigation and Post-Disaster Aid

From the point of view of the property owner, insurance, mitigation, and post-disaster aid are all substitutes, providing either funds to cover losses or lowering losses contingent on a natural disaster event occurring. As noted by a number of authors, establishment of public subsidies for insurance or mitigation, or the provision of post-disaster relief have the effect of shifting the burden of loss, both loss expected *ex ante* and loss experienced *ex post*, from the property holder to others. Unsubsidized insurance shifts the burden of loss *ex post* to those entities who have purchased the contingent liability but not *ex post* as actuarially sound premiums reflect expectations of loss. These issues are part of current public policy debates regarding the establishment or extension of government insurance programs and requirements for mitigation in the form of zoning. Another response has been the Costal Barriers Resources Act of 1982 which prohibits federal government programs, including the NFIP, from activity in areas designated as part of the Costal Barriers Resources System (CBRS). New development in such areas is totally dependent on private funding for infrastructure, mitigation, and insurance. This has led to the curious situation in which, along a given beach, successive areas are full participants in NFIP and beach nourishment programs while neighboring areas rely entirely on private sector development and insurance. The expectation that government subsidized insurance and mitigation followed by post-disaster aid will lead to over-development and under mitigation in high risk areas is largely based on partial equilibrium models in which the expected cost of hazard events born by property owners is reduced by the subsidy.

There is some empirical evidence in Schilling, Sirmans, and Benjamin (1984), that subsidized insurance is capitalized into land values. This is consistent with Frame's (1998) general equilibrium result that insurance subsidies raise land prices, house prices, and the physical density of development, while the effect of insurance subsidies on the density of population in high risk areas is ambiguous, except that some areas previously considered too risky for development are developed. Cordes and Yezer (1998) test directly for the empirical effects of subsidized insurance through the NFIP, and mitigation, in the form of beach enhancement by the U.S. Army Corps of Engineers (Corps). They estimate a model of beachfront residential development, specifically the rate at which new building permits are issued, for a panel of beach communities that allows for the observation of communities with and without insurance and enhancement programs and also observation of given communities before and after programs were implemented. The results suggest that provision of subsidized insurance under the NFIP encouraged higher levels of real estate development in beachfront communities. However, subsidized mitigation in the form of U.S. Army Corps of Engineers beach enhancement had no such effect on development. These results may appear surprising because only a modest fraction of property owners in beachfront communities chose to maintain insurance in force. Nevertheless, insurance availability appears to have encouraged new construction while beach enhancement failed to do so. Overall, a number of papers have produced theoretical results suggesting that provision of subsidized insurance or mitigation efforts tends to increase the density of real property development in high hazard areas. The implications of insurance for both development and mitigation in such a general equilibrium setting have been neglected along with the implications of post-disaster aid. Finally, there is little empirical evidence on the size of these real estate development effects. The effects of insurance availability and/or public mitigation efforts on the decision to develop high hazard areas are clearly important and should be the object of additional testing. The interaction between development and mitigation efforts and the provision of post-disaster aid is well recognized as an important policy concern but has not been the object of substantial formal modeling. A number of authors, including Rubin (1982), have noted that systematic withholding of disaster relief from individuals who have failed to mitigate risks is not politically credible. Most disaster relief schemes clearly include a measure of equity and efficiency for reasons discussed in Dacy and Kunreuther (1969).

These implicit equity-efficiency tradeoffs have been examined explicitly by Butler and Doessel (1981) and a scheme for partial loss compensation, with the replacement rate varying inversely with income, developed as a remedy. The full set of tradeoffs among *ex post* disaster relief expenditures and *ex ante* decisions regarding development and mitigation expenditures, was developed by Lewis and Nickerson (1989). In this model, risk averse households living in areas varying in hazard risk can invest either in risky structures or in risk preventing mitigation. While "expected" findings of excess spending on risky structures and under-investment in mitigation in the presence of disaster relief are obtained from this model, the results are complex. Mitigation expenditures designed to prevent small losses are undertaken because those losses do not result in aid but there is underspending on efforts to avoid substantial losses where relief is expected. The authors conclude with a list of potential research extensions that are still waiting to be made.

## Design of Financial Instruments for Capitalizing Private Insurance

In addition to the concern expressed by Kunreuther (1978, 1996) and others that property owners fail to demand actuarially fair insurance against hazard losses, there is also concern with the supply side of the See Kunreuther and Roth (1998) for a discussion of hazard insurance regulation and subsidies including the California Earthquake Authority and the Florida Joint Underwriting Authority. hazard insurance market. Insurance markets normally provide policies in which the price of coverage reflects differential risks of loss plus a margin for normal returns and administrative costs. Companies maintain sufficient capital to cover expected losses and, in periods where losses are high, are able to raise additional capital at moderate cost. Private insurance should price risk appropriately and provide incentives for deterring investment in high-risk areas and for mitigation efforts, in the form of reduced premiums. A number of sources, including the Congressional Research Service (1992) and Kunreuther and Roth (1998) have noted that private insurance markets have failed to perform this function for property owners in areas with high hazard risks. Nine smaller insurance companies failed in the wake of hurricane Andrew while others tried to reduce coverage or asked for increased premiums. The public sector response was to insist on continuing coverage at current rates. Clearly neither the initial structure of the market nor the regulatory response fit the normal insurance market model. In response to the problems faced by private insurance companies providing coverage in areas where expected hazard events are particularly severe, a recent literature has considered innovative financial instruments and changes in tax law that could provide substantial capital for companies supplying disaster insurance. Problems identified in the current system as noted by Cummins and Geman (1995), Lewis and Murdock (1996), and Jaffee and Russel (1997), arise from the extraordinary payouts of claims in excess of the flow of premium revenues. These payouts produce periods of negative cash flow and profits which reduce the accumulated capital reserves of insurance companies when major disaster events occur. Four possible solutions to this problem have been considered. Obviously, premium rates must be sufficient to cover expected losses plus normal profits and administrative costs. Second, private reinsurance markets could be further developed to better diversify risk across the nation and even the world. Third, tax law changes could delay recognition of profit on insurance against natural disaster events by substituting a multi-year accounting period for the current annual period used to compute taxable income. Actuarially fair insurance will generate apparently large accounting profits over short periods followed by large losses when disasters occur. Unfortunately, it may be difficult for insurance firms to recapitalize after particularly large losses even if they have tax advantages associated with a large loss carry forward. While corporate profits taxes may appear to diversify some of the risk of large claims to the government, the very uneven nature of disaster losses appears to reduce the value of the diversification benefits. The fourth solution to the capitalization problem has captured recent attention and involves the design of contingent liabilities whose value depends on the amount of disaster claims losses in any given period. Purchasers of such liabilities earn high returns in periods where claims are negligible and low or even negative returns when major disaster events produce high claims rates.

This line of inquiry has been spurred by specific attempts in the private sector to develop new instruments including "Act of God" bonds, and catastrophe futures and options. Jaffee and Russell (1997) note that accounting requirements, tax provisions, takeover threats against firms with large cash surplus, and regulatory constraints all limit insurance company capital held for catastrophes. Nevertheless they argue that primary problems of disaster insurance reside in capital markets and that some form of government sponsored reinsurance may be required. In order not to crowd out private sector innovations, the government reinsurance program would only apply to disaster events in which aggregate losses exceeded some substantial threshold, say twenty billion dollars. Overall, the ability of insurance markets to serve areas subject to large scale disaster losses is an active topic of research involving both insurance and capital market issues.

## Empirical Models of Economic Impacts of Disaster Events

These models trace the likely economic effects of a disaster event. In contrast to the theoretical models of effects on housing markets and residential real estate development, these models emphasize effects on industrial output, although effects of rebuilding of the residential capital stock are usually included. The effects of disasters are generated by simulating a base line economic scenario and then comparing this with one or more disaster event scenarios. The appropriate comparison is economic activity with and without the disaster event. It is important to model effects so that all costs can be measured without double counting. For example, it is a model should estimate both the cost of damaged property and subsequent output loss due to inoperable equipment, However, it is not appropriate to add both the value of damaged equipment and costs of replacing that damaged equipment. A model should also be capable of estimating costs over time because a cost experienced today is worth more than a cost years after the disaster event. Finally, it is important to distinguish positive models of the most likely effects of a disaster and normative models that attempt to reallocate resources in the post-disaster period in order to minimize losses.

There are two distinct modeling approaches, regional econometric models and inter-industry (input-output) models. In either case, some special adaptations of the standard regional model are necessary if it is to be used for estimating effects of disasters. Specifically, disasters lower subsequent output levels by disrupting the availability of inputs locally and the ability to transport inputs from alternative locations. Most regional econometric and input-output models are designed to estimate the effects of fluctuations in national demand for regional products on regional output assuming that input supplies are very elastic. Therefore, modeling effects of supply disruptions as well as efforts to rebuild damaged local capital stock requires some special adaptation of the usual model.

Ellison, Milliman, and Roberts (1984) used regional econometric model to study regional disaster impacts. Regional econometric models consist of a series of equations characterizing output, usually disaggregated by a few broad sectors, employment, consumption, labour supply, wages, and prices with additional specialized modules, often including local government and housing. In order to capture the effects of natural disasters on local economic activity, the econometric model should include equations reflecting the process of local investment and capital stock accumulation and then relate local output levels to both capital and labor inputs. Special attention to residential real estate production and accumulation is also needed if the recovery process is to be modeled. The model should allow both labour migration and local capital investment decisions to be modified by expectations in response to disaster events. It is also important to include a role for transfers from private insurance and public disaster aid. The regional econometric model is usually estimated using annual data often available for only 30 or 40 years. With so few observations, the complexity of individual equations is limited. Ellison, Milliman and Roberts (1984) argue that it is important to disaggregate the region into subareas when disaster events are localized within an urban area. Data are available to disaggregate Metropolitan Statistical Areas by county. Overall, substantial modification of traditional regional econometric models is necessary if these models are to be used in disaster impact evaluation. A guide to these needed modifications along with practical suggestions for their achievement in the face of data limitations has been provided by West and Lenze (1994). Regional interindustry models are traditionally demand driven with in changes exogenous national demand for regional exports drive the local economy. However, these models can been substantially modified to include supply side feedback effects and their superior industrial disaggregation allows them to trace specific interindustry effects of supply disruptions. Earlier examples of the adaptation of inputoutput approaches include Cochrane (1974) and Rose (1991). An regional input-output modeling effort requires that the extent of local interdependence among industries be identified. The extent to which local industries rely on inputs of locally produced intermediate product is made apparent in the modeling process. Accordingly, the output effects of an interruption of these sources of local supply can be determined. Of course, it is difficult to determine the effect of a disaster on the availability of inputs imported from outside the area to replace local supplies. But the input-output model can be used to estimate the effects of local supply interruptions under alternative assumptions on the availability of imports.

It is also possible to adapt inter-industry models to an optimizing mode and to draw implications for the effect of alternative post-disaster responses on local output. The optimizing model works to achieve an allocation of infrastructure inputs to minimize the output effects of disruption. This literature has reached very sophisticated levels with models such as Rose *et al.* (1997) in which programming models are used to allocate scarce electricity disrupted by a disaster event. This model is remarkable to the extent of geographic disaggregation which allows for the simulation of effects of electricity outages at the substation level. The model operates in normative mode to identify patterns of electricity restoration that minimize the loss of local value added in the post-disaster period.

Although there is a tendency to think of using economic impact models to estimate the likely losses from disaster events, their greatest value may be in simulating the effects of alternative approaches to post-disaster recovery.

Two conclusions emerge from the above is review. First, the economic effects of natural disasters is a remarkably under researched area. The total number of citations to research in economics of disasters is very small and the number of potential topics is quite large, leaving a very thin rate of coverage. Second, various approaches to the economics of disasters have remained segregated. Theoretical models including information effects have had little effect on economic impact modeling. There are few empirical tests of information effects. The relation among insurance, mitigation, and post-disaster relief has been examined but the exploration is far from complete. One branch of literature has concentrated on the response of households and residential housing markets while the economic impact literature has dealt largely with firms.

## Section IV

## NATURAL CATASTROPHE MODELING

Natural catastrophe modeling is a risk management tool that uses computer technology to help insurers, reinsurers and risk managers better assess the potential losses caused by natural and man-made catastrophes. Natural catastrophe models combine historical disaster information with current demographic, building (age, type and usage), scientific and financial data to determine the potential cost of catastrophes for a specified geographic area. The models use these vast databases of information to simulate the physical characteristics of thousands of potential catastrophes and project their effects on both residential and commercial property.

The modeling process evolved in the late 1980s as the insurance companies became increasingly aware of their exposure to catastrophic risks. After Hurricane Andrew in 1992 and the Northridge earthquake in 1994, the use of catastrophe models took off as companies sought to more accurately analyze, write and price for natural catastrophe risk.

Natural catastrophe models have since been developed for a wide range of catastrophic risks and geographic territories worldwide, including specific industry types. All major natural hazards are modeled, including hurricanes, earthquakes, winter storms, tornadoes, hailstorms and floods. Today, the three main proprietary catastrophe modeling firms are: Applied Insurance Research (AIR) Worldwide, Risk Management Solutions (RMS) and EQECAT (also known as EQE). Major insurance and reinsurance brokers such as Aon, Benfield, Guy Carpenter and Willis license models from these firms and also develop their own models to assist their direct clients and primary insurers. Some academic institutions and at least one state (Florida) have also developed models.

The process of developing sophisticated catastrophe models is complex and draws on expertise from a broad range of technical and financial disciplines. The models utilize the skills of many experts, including meteorologists, seismologists, geologists, engineers, mathematicians, actuaries, decision scientists and statisticians.

Over the years, catastrophe models have been constantly updated and fine-tuned to incorporate the latest technologies, data, and research findings. For example, some of the latest models are increasingly incorporating scientific and economic data, such as changing weather patterns and the impact on claim costs of surging material and labor prices after events occur. Catastrophe models will continue to evolve amid the ever-changing risk landscape.

Catastrophe models can help insurers, reinsurers and risk managers to determine the most accurate risk management and pricing strategies. In this way, catastrophe models help to ensure that individual companies have sufficient resources to withstand one or more major disasters.

Models incorporate financial data from insurers and reinsurers, such as the value of insured property, deductibles or attachment points, and policy limits, to create a profile of the probability of loss from different event scenarios exceeding certain (dollar) levels. Companies can evaluate the correlation of expected losses from a single event or combination of events affecting more than one territory. In this way catastrophe models assist insurers in the management of their aggregate catastrophe exposure.

With these model outputs, underwriters are better equipped to analyze and evaluate the overall level of capital required to support a portfolio and to allocate capital between the individual risks within that portfolio. Model outputs are also an important component of the catastrophe analysis and "stress testing" conducted by rating agencies as they assess the financial strength of insurance companies. The ability of insurers to withstand multiple catastrophic events is an area of increased scrutiny by ratings organizations and regulators.

Insurers cannot arbitrarily raise rates based on catastrophe model outputs. When included as part of a rating plan by insurers, catastrophe models are subject to approval by state insurance regulators.

### Catastrophe Modeling Post-Hurricane Katrina

Following the unprecedented frequency and severity of storms during the 2004 and 2005 hurricane seasons, catastrophe models have faced some criticism within the industry for underestimating the losses. Additionally, many insurance regulators remain reluctant to permit their widespread use, often alleging that they are "black boxes".

Limiting the use of models or failing to adjust them for recent experience will add greater uncertainty to the already difficult decisions of which properties insurers and reinsurers can underwrite and at what price. The end result would be to make insurers and reinsurers more reluctant to provide coverage in catastrophe-prone areas.

It is important to recognize that there are a number of different methodological approaches to catastrophe modeling, each using somewhat different assumptions, data inputs and computational algorithms. Models are used not just by insurers, but also by weather forecasters and government agencies. Consequently, the output of competing models while generally consistent will vary and estimated losses will contain some deviation from actual observed losses. Additional uncertainty also arises from the simple random deviation observed in all complex meteorological or geological processes.

Just as insurers and reinsurers are constantly reassessing their risks, so too are catastrophe modeling companies continually reviewing, updating and refining their models. The fruits of these efforts will lead to improved model accuracy and detail across a broad spectrum of catastrophic loss scenarios worldwide.

There is, however, one thing all experts seem to agree on: for whatever reason, water temperatures in the Gulf and Atlantic Ocean are rising and, as a result, more frequent and more severe storms are expected. At the same time, more Americans have moved to coastal areas vulnerable to catastrophic hurricanes.

Catastrophe modeling is just one tool in the risk management box available to insurers and reinsurers as they look to better manage and prepare for disasters in the years to come. Everyone insurers, home owners, businesses and government have a stake in being better prepared to protect lives, property and financial security in this increasingly hazardous environment.

## Assessment of Extreme Losses from Natural Disasters : The AIR Approach

Natural disasters fortunately, are rare events. That means, however, that assessing and quantifying potential losses from future natural disasters is a difficult task given the limited loss information that is available from past events. A quick look at the top natural disasters in recent decades reveals that earthquakes and cyclones, both tropical and extratropical, are the perils that contribute most to losses worldwide. The Applied Insurance Research Inc, U.S.A. (AIR) has developed a natural disaster loss estimation methodology for assessing risk arising from these three perils. AIR natural catastrophe models simulate the physical characteristics of natural hazards and project their effects on property, including residential, commercial and industrial facilities, and automobiles.

AIR scientists and engineers have developed these sophisticated computer models for all major natural hazards, including hurricanes, earthquakes, extratropical cyclones (winter storms), tornadoes, hailstorms and flood, for more than 40 countries throughout North America, the Caribbean, South America, Europe and the Asia-Pacific region.

AIR models undergo a continual process of review and refinement. They incorporate the latest technologies, data, and research findings in seismology, meteorology, hydrodynamics, structural and geotechnical engineering. AIR models are meticulously validated at every stage of development and model results are calibrated using data from historical events. Simulated event characteristics parallel patterns observed in the historical record and resulting loss estimates correspond closely to actual claims data provided by client companies. Internal peer review is standard operating procedure at AIR. AIR models also undergo extensive external review. AIR's recently introduced Advanced Component Method (ACM) is a ground-breaking methodology for assessing building vulnerability to earthquakes.

## Natural Disaster Loss Estimation Methodology

Through the application of a stochastic simulation process, AIR natural disaster loss estimation methodology involves estimating the probability that events of particular intensities will occur. In the next step, the potential financial loss to a property/building or a portfolio of buildings as a percentage of the replacement value of the building is estimated. From an insurance perspective, the estimated loss is the sum of loss to the building, the contents and time element loss (that is, expenses associated with the loss of use in the case of residential properties and with business interruption in the case of commercial properties). Figure 6 below illustrates the various components of the natural disaster risk analysis model. All the AIR models for each peril and region follow this generic framework.

FIG. 6

**Natural Disaster Model Components (in gray)**

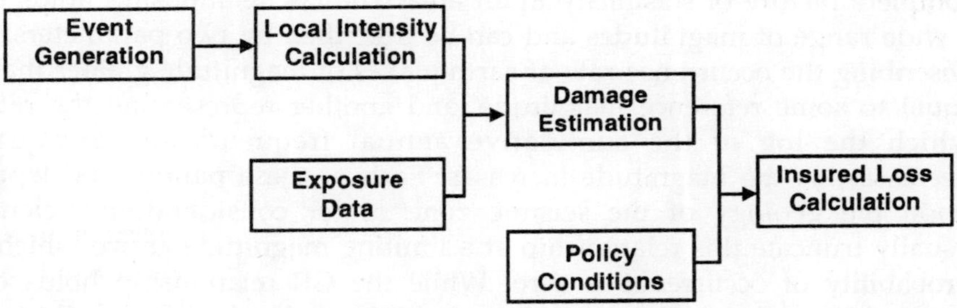


*Source* : Jayanta Guin and Vinita Saxena (2007): "Extreme Losses From Natural Disasters—Earthquakes, Tropical Cyclones and Extratropical Cyclones", www.air-worldwide.com/public/html/pubspc.asp.

## Event Generation and Local Intensity

The event generation component of the models determines the frequency, magnitude, and other characteristics of potential natural disaster events by geographic location. This requires, among other things, a thorough analysis of the characteristics of historical events as well as an understanding of the region-specific features, whether seismotectonic, geological, topographical, or atmospheric, those are likely to influence the behavior of future natural disaster events.

Natural disaster models can vary in their approach to event generation. Some are parameterized models, as in the case of the earthquake and tropical cyclone models discussed here. Others are physical models; that are more appropriate for capturing complex phenomena, such as extratropical cyclones. Table 4 summarizes the difference among the model components for the three perils chosen in this study.

All natural disaster events are complex and their characterization requires the use of large numbers of variables. In the case of the parameterized models, event generation begins by collecting the available scientific data pertaining to these variables from many different sources. The data are cleaned and verified. After a rigorous data analysis, researchers develop probability distributions for each of the variables, testing them for goodness-of-fit and robustness. The selection and subsequent refinement of these distributions are based on statistical techniques, on well-established scientific principles and on an understanding of how catastrophic events behave. The resulting distributions are used to produce a large catalog of simulated events. That is, by sampling from these distributions, the model generates simulated "years' of event activity. Many thousands of these scenario years are then generated to produce a stochastic catalog that represents the complete and stable range of potential natural disaster event activity. Seismologists typically fit historical data on the frequency and magnitude of earthquakes to an exponential distribution called the Gutenberg-Richter (GR) relationship. The GR relationship applies globally and allows an extrapolation from the limited historical record to estimate a more complete picture of seismicity in an area. The GR relationship holds over a wide range of magnitudes and can be described by two parameters: one describing the occurrence rate of earthquakes of magnitude greater than or equal to some reference magnitude, and another representing the rate at which the log of the cumulative annual frequency of earthquakes decreases, as the magnitude increases. Each of these parameters depends upon the geology of the seismic zone under consideration. Scientists usually truncate this relationship at a limiting magnitude above which the probability of occurrence is zero. While the GR relationship holds on a regional or global scale, it may not hold for individual faults. For some seismic zones, there exists evidence that earthquakes of a certain magnitude occur with a frequency that is not consistent with the rate

TABLE 4

**The Methodological Approach to the Model Components**

| *Event Generation Peril* | *Parameterized * Historical Data * Geophysical and Geodetic data Earthquake* | *Parameterized *Historical Data *Metereological expertise Tropical Cyclone* | *Physical *Global reanalysis data * Numerical Weather Prediction Extratropiic* |
|---|---|---|---|
| (1) | (2) | (3) | (4) |
| Local Intensity | Attenuation Relationships Spectral Ordinates | Empirical Metereological Equations Wind Speed time profile | Engineering studies, structural calculations, expert opinion and post-disaster surveys claims data |
| Damage | Engineering Analysis based on Objective Methodology ACM | Engineering studies, structural calculations, expert opinion and post-disaster surveys Claims data | |

*Source* : Jayanta Guin and Vinita Saxena (2007): "Extreme Losses From Natural Disasters-Earthquakes, Tropical Cyclones and Extratropical Cyclones", www.air-worldwide.com/_public/html/pubspc.asp.

predicted by the GR relationship. Scientists now believe that many faults tend to produce repeated earthquakes of a size that is "characteristic" of that particular fault or fault segment. In general, plate margin earthquakes associated with subduction zone regions, such as along the East Coast of Japan are modeled primarily as characteristic events. Known active crustal faults are modeled using a weighted combination of characteristic earthquakes and seismicity as generated by the Gutenberg-Richter relationship. Finally, a smoothed background seismicity distribution is used to capture the small to moderate events that could occur as a result of as yet unknown or unmapped faults.Some of the other key earthquake model variables include depth, rupture length, azimuth, dip angle and rupture mechanism. After the model generates the location, magnitude, and other fundamental characteristics of the simulated earthquake, it calculates intensity at each location affected by the event. To do this, the model uses attenuation relationships, which mathematically describe the rate at which the amplitude of the seismic waves decreases as the waves propagate outward from the source of the rupture. The shaking intensity derived from these attenuation relationships is then modified to reflect specific local site conditions such as ground motion amplification and soil liquefaction. In the case of tropical cyclones, some of the primary model variables are the annual frequency, landfall location, minimum central pressure, radius of maximum wind, forward speed, track angle at landfall and the storm track. The available historical data pertaining to chosen parameters is collected and probability distributions for each of these parameters are derived based on historical data combined with meteorological expertise. For example, the model uses a weibull distribution for the central pressure, lognormal distribution for forward speed and a normal distribution for the radius of maximum wind in Florida hurricane. The local wind speed profile for each simulated event is calculated using empirical meteorological equations with adjustments made for asymmetry effects, storm filling over land and surface friction. The model developed for extratropical cyclones, is not a traditional parameterized model, but is a physical model that employs, Numerical Weather Prediction (NWP) techniques. Such models can capture the evolution of a storm due to small changes in the initial conditions of the atmosphere. This attribute is leveraged in the event generation by perturbing, both temporally and spatially, the initial conditions of a set of "seed" storms drawn from the historical data. NWP models use global environmental data such as sea surface temperatures, wind speed and pressure in conjunction with governing equations based on known physical laws, to model the evolution of circulation patterns in three dimensional space. The data are used to define the "state-of-the-atmosphere variables" (SAVS). The process begins with an initial three-dimensional field of these SAVS flow, that is, an initial snapshot at the surface and at multiple upper atmospheric layers. Because the motion of air depends on the pressure gradient, from this pressure field a windfield is generated. The wind field of each of these perturbed seed storms is then moved forward in time through the application of a set of partial differential equations governing fluid that have, as their basis, the law of conservation of mass and energy.

## Vulnerability/Damage Estimation

Vulnerability relationships or damage functions relate the mean damage as well as the variability of damage to the measure of intensity. They implicitly describe the interaction between buildings, both their structural and non-structural components as well as their contents, and the local intensity to which they are exposed. Because different structural types experience varying degrees of damage, the vulnerability relationships are developed according by construction types and occupancy. In the model, damage is expressed by means of a damage ratio between the repair cost of the damaged property and the replacement value of the property. The probability distribution of damage is calculated by applying the appropriate function to the replacement value of the property. Damage to buildings from earthquakes is both structural and non-structural in nature and can be modeled using certain objective parameters such as inter-story drift, base shear, ductility ratio, etc. For earthquakes, structural damage can be extremely severe even for engineered buildings. This was the case for Kobe earthquake in Japan, where the seismic building codes are considered to be one of the most advanced in the world. On the other hand, damage due to wind is primarily non-structural, involving different components of the building envelope and, in most cases, is localized in nature. Under extreme wind events, even if structural collapse occurs, it is usually restricted to non-engineered buildings such as wood frames. Due to the lack of test data on component or envelope resistances, most of present day knowledge of wind damage comes from damage investigations conducted in the aftermath of an event. Recourse is frequently made to engineering experience and knowledge to develop vulnerability functions for wind induced damage. In the AIR model for earthquakes, building vulnerability to ground shaking is developed using a rigorous engineering-based methodology known as ACM (Advanced Component Method) which uses spectral displacement (Sd) as a measure of earthquake intensity. In the case of wind damage from tropical and extratropical cyclones, the model vulnerability relationships are based on engineering studies, structural calculations and expert opinion. The resulting relationships are extensively validated using actual claims data obtained from insurance companies for various windstorm events. Fortunately, windstorm events are quite frequent and hence sufficient data is available to perform these validations at detailed geographic resolutions. In the model, based on the local intensity calculated for each simulated event, the corresponding damage estimates for exposed property are obtained from the associated vulnerability relationship. The damage estimates are translated into monetary losses due to direct structural and non-structural damage and due to business interruption. The final output of the natural disaster loss model is the probability distributions for losses. Output from the model can be easily customized to any desired degree of geographical resolution down to location level, by construction class, aggregation of property classes, etc.

## SECTION V

## INSURANCE AGAINST NATURAL DISASTER

### The U.S. Scenario

In the U.S., the property insurance companies provide insurance against catastrophe. The term "catastrophe" in the property insurance industry denotes a natural or man-made disaster that is unusually severe and that affects many insurers and policy-holders. An event is designated a catastrophe when claims are expected to reach a certain dollar threshold, currently set at $ 25 million.

The typical homeowners insurance policy covers damage from a fire, windstorms, hail, riots and explosions as well as other types of loss such as theft and the cost of living elsewhere while the structure is being repaired or rebuilt after being damaged. Commercial property insurance policies generally cover the same causes of loss with some variation, depending on the coverage selected. Flood and earthquake damage are excluded under homeowners policies separate policies are available but are covered under the comprehensive portion of the standard auto policy, which more than 75 percent of drivers who buy auto liability insurance purchase.

Over the 20-year period, 1986 to 2005, hurricanes and tropical storms made up 47.5 percent of total catastrophe losses, followed by tornado losses (24.5 percent), winter storms (7.8 percent), terrorism (7.7 percent), earthquakes and other geologic events (6.7 percent), wind/hail/flood (2.8 percent) and fire (2.3 percent). Civil disorders, water damage and utility services disruption combined represented less than 1 percent. Each year about 7 percent of homeowners file a homeowners insurance claim, according to ISO.

The insurance industry tracks catastrophes to monitor claim costs, assigning a number to each catastrophe. Each claim arising from the event is tagged so that total industry wide losses can be tabulated. The term catastrophe is often used in the property insurance industry in a narrow way to mean a catastrophic event that exceeds a dollar threshold in claims payouts. This figure has changed over the years with inflation and the increase in development of areas subject to natural disasters. Thus, beginning in 1997 when the catastrophe definition was raised from $5 million to $25 million in insured damage, the number of recorded

TABLE 5

**Most Costly Natural Disasters in the U.S.**

| *Rank* | *Date* | *Name* | *Dollars When Occurred* |
|---|---|---|---|
| 1 | Aug. 2005 | Hurricane Katrina | $41,100 |
| 2 | Aug. 1992 | Hurricane Andrew | 15,500 |
| 3 | Jan. 1994 | Northridge, CA earthquake | 12,500 |
| 4 | Oct. 2005 | Hurricane Wilma | 10,300 |
| 5 | Aug. 2004 | Hurricane Charley | 7,475 |
| 6 | Sep. 2004 | Hurricane Ivan | 7,110 |
| 7 | Sep. 1989 | Hurricane Hugo | 4,195 |
| 8 | Sep. 2005 | Hurricane Rita | 5,627 |
| 9 | Sep. 2004 | Hurricane Frances | 4,595 |

*Source* : ISO's Property Claim Services unit; Insurance Information Institute.

catastrophes and the aggregate losses attributed to catastrophes on average is lower than in earlier years.

## Catastrophe Deductibles

After Hurricane Andrew, with computer-based models of storms, coastal development patterns and increasing values all indicating how vulnerable insurers were to large weather-related losses, homeowners insurers had difficulty finding the reinsurance coverage they needed to protect their own bottom line. Many homeowners insurers couldn't obtain reinsurance coverage unless they agreed to greatly reduce their potential maximum losses from such events through higher deductibles. These deductibles exist in regions prone to hail as well as hurricane damage. They are generally equal to a percentage of the structure's insured value as opposed to a straight dollar amount, such as $1,000. Eighteen states and the District of Columbia have what have become known as hurricane deductibles.

Percentage deductibles for windstorm losses, which may be mandatory in some coastal areas of a state, vary from 1 percent of the home's insured value to 15 percent, depending on many factors that differ from state to state, and sometimes from insurer to insurer, including the home's insured value and the "trigger", the nature of the event to which the deductible applies. In some states or portions of a state, policyholders have a "buy-back" option paying a higher premium in return for a traditional dollar rather than percentage deductible. The percentage deductibles may apply to the entire state or just part of it.

For hail damage, in addition to instituting percentage of limits deductibles, some insurers in some states are providing coverage for roofs on a depreciated (actual cash value) basis, rather than replacing a damaged roof with a new one. Some insurers are offering a discount for hail resistive roofs or imposing a surcharge for roofs that are not hail resistive to encourage people to replace old roofs with new less damageable ones.

## Earthquakes

On the West Coast, earthquakes represent the greatest threat A major earthquake (8.2 on the Richter scale) in San Francisco today could cause as much as $84 billion in damage. However, a major earthquake on the East Coast, though more unlikely, could. Statistics show that since 1900, earthquakes have occurred in 39 states and have caused damage in all 50. About 5,000 quakes can be felt each year, with some 400 capable of causing damage to the interior of buildings and 20 capable of causing structural damage.cause much greater damage. Because earthquakes in the eastern part of the country tend to be thrust-fault quakes, which produce an up-and-down motion rather than the horizontal side-to-side common in California, damage could be 10 times greater, according to seismic experts. The degree of damage also depends on other variables such as the structure of the building and soil conditions.

A study by Dr. Haresh Shah of Risk Management Solutions and Stanford University, which draws on data from the 1994 Northridge quake and the 1995 quake in Kobe, Japan, suggests the ground shaking at a quake's epicenter can be more violent than expected. This finding has pushed up earlier estimates for loss of life and property damage in the event of a megaquake. An 8.3 magnitude quake in San Francisco, the same in intensity as the quake in 1906, could cause up to 8,000 deaths and between $80 and $105 billion in insured losses, with total losses as high as $225 billion. (Total damage from the Kobe, Japan, quake was $147 billion, of which only $4.1 billion was insured.) New estimates of the potential damage to Tokyo in a major earthquake are numbing. A quake similar to the one that destroyed the city in 1923 could cause as much as $4.3 trillion in total losses.

## Earthquake Insurance

California insurers collected only $3.4 billion in earthquake premiums in the 25-year period prior to the Northridge earthquake and paid out more than $15.3 billion on Northridge claims alone. After the Northridge earthquake, insurers were reluctant to offer homeowners insurance because they feared additional earthquake exposure could potentially bankrupt them. In response to this crisis in the homeowners insurance market, in 1995 California lawmakers passed a two-part bill that allowed insurers to offer a new earthquake policy with a maximum deductible of 15 percent and created a privately funded, state-run earthquake pool.

Insurers doing business in California must offer earthquake insurance to their homeowners insurance policyholders, either a policy from the California Earthquake Authority (CEA) or, if they do not participate in the pool, a policy that they underwrite. Several dozen companies now write earthquake insurance in California in addition to the CEA. The CEA became operational in December 1996, with a $10.5 billion funding package. The CEA could now pay claims caused by a quake more than twice as destructive as Northridge since with each passing earthquake-free year, its claims paying ability increases. Passage of the CEA legislation opened up the homeowners market (see Earthquake paper). More recently, the CEA created a supplementary policy to broaden coverage. Nevertheless, only a small portion of the state's property owners buy earthquake insurance and the percentage appears to grow smaller as the time span since the last major quake increases.

Tornadoes: Each year, about 1,200 tornadoes with gusts of wind as high as 200 mph touch down in the United States. Tornado intensity is measured by the Fujita scale which runs from 0 through 5, the most damaging, based on the maximum speed of three-second wind gusts and the potential for damage. Though generally not as costly in terms of insured values as hurricanes because they strike a more limited geographic area, tornadoes are more frequent. They can cause severe damage and, particularly before the advent of tornado warnings, many deaths. In the decade, 1965-74, they were responsible for an average of 141 deaths each year, compared with 62 in the 10 years 1997-2006. The peak of the tornado season is April through June or July. Spring tornadoes tend to be more severe and strike the Southeast, which is more densely populated than the Great Plains, thus causing more deaths than those in the summer months. In addition, the South has more mobile homes than other regions. Mobile homes are vulnerable to tornado damage.

Since 1990 the number of tornadoes has generally exceeded 1,000 a year. In the three preceding decades, the only year in which there were more than 1,000 tornadoes was 1973, when 1,102 were reported. This increase may reflect greater ability to detect tornadoes.

## Wildland Fires

Fire plays an important role in the life of a forest, clearing away dead wood and undergrowth to make way for younger trees. But for much of the last century, fire-suppression policies focused on extinguishing wildfires as quickly as possible to preserve timber and, increasingly, real estate. These policies have led to the accumulation of brush and other vegetation that is easily ignited and serves as fuel for wildfires. In an effort to reduce the incidence of wildfires, increasingly fire officials are promoting "prescribed burns" to eliminate the accumulated debris. In recent years, most of the large fires with significant property damage have occurred in California, where some of the fastest developing counties are in forested areas. However, wildfires are a growing threat in other states, particularly when there is a drought, as more homes are built in woodland areas that were once wild.

Fire damage is covered under a homeowners insurance policy whatever the cause of the fire unless the person insured under the policy commits arson by intentionally setting fire to the structure. As a result of the greater potential for fire losses where homes are built on mountainous and forested sites, insurers are increasingly requiring homeowners whose property is at risk to take precautions to slow the spread of fire. Such measures include installing fire resistant roofs and creating a "defensible zone" around the home by removing debris, overhanging tree branches and other items located close to the building that can become fuel for a fire.

## Reinsurance

Just as individuals and businesses buy insurance to protect their assets, primary insurers, the companies that sell insurance to consumers, buy reinsurance to protect their bottom line. Reinsurance is sold in layers, reaching up into the millions of dollars to protect insurance companies from possible, but statistically highly unlikely events such as a $100 million court award or an extraordinary number of homeowners claims as a result of a hurricane or a fast-spreading bush fire.

Retentions and coinsurance, through which insurers share the risk at various levels with their reinsurers, as well as coverage amounts, have increased dramatically over the past decade. It is now patently evident that the cost of catastrophes, both natural and man-made, can be in the tens of billions of dollars. Hurricane Katrina cost more than $40 billion but a hurricane hit to Miami or a major terrorist attack could cost much more.

## Pricing

The price of an insurance policy reflects the costs of paying claims covered by that policy, as well as an insurance company's costs for such items as reinsurance. Not surprisingly, reinsurance costs as well as direct claims costs are lower where the risk is low. For example, if a community has a good fire department and ready access to water to extinguish fires, serious fires in that community will likely be fewer than in similar communities that lack a good fire department. The same principle applies to windstorms: premiums will reflect the normal level of windstorm claims in a given community.

Prior to Hurricane Andrew, insurance companies accounted for hurricanes and other catastrophes with a special premium amount known as a "catastrophe loading" to spread the risk over a period spanning 30 to 40 years. Sometimes they used data from several states subject to the same kind of catastrophes to develop the average annual cost of catastrophes. However, since the mid-1990s more sophisticated computer modeling techniques have become available. Insurers now base their rates on sophisticated computer models that combine meteorological data with their own exposure data. The meteorological data show the probability of a natural disaster occurring in a particular geographical area and the exposure data indicate how many of the company's policyholders are likely to be affected and to what extent, i.e., what the insurer's potential losses from that event are likely to be.

## Special Catastrophe Programs

In the United States special pools, known as Beach and Windstorm Plans, ensure the availability of windstorm insurance for properties close to the ocean. These pools, which exist in seven states along the Gulf and Atlantic coasts in various forms, are operated by property insurers doing business in the state, and in some cases by the state itself. Hawaii created a fund but this was disbanded in December 2000.

## Flood Insurance

Flood damage is excluded under homeowners policies, but it is covered under the comprehensive section of standard auto insurance policies and some coverage is available for floods under special commercial insurance policies. Some insurance companies provide coverage under homeowners policies for the backup of sewers and drains and some companies offer flood coverage to homeowners to augment coverage provided by the National Flood Insurance Program.

Flood insurance for homeowners and businesses is available from the federal government. The private sector cannot insure widespread floods because only people concentrated in flood-prone zones would purchase flood insurance and those people would have frequent claims, making the coverage prohibitively expensive. Before Congress passed the National Flood Insurance Act in 1968, after Mississippi River flooding, the national response to flood disasters had been to build dams, levees and other structures to hold back flood waters, a policy that may have encouraged building in flood zones.

The National Flood Insurance Act was amended in 1969 to provide coverage for mudslides and again in 1973. This last amendment put constraints on the use of federal funds in flood plain areas unless the property was protected by flood insurance, a provision that was expected to make coverage in flood plains almost universal. No lenders that are federally insured or financed can lend money on a property in a flood plain zone when a community is participating in the National Flood Insurance Program (NFIP) unless the property is covered by flood insurance. However, because the initial mortgage on the property is frequently sold by the originating bank to another entity, enforcement of this law has been poor.

Flood insurance is only available where the local government bodies have adopted adequate flood plain management regulations for their flood plain areas under the NFIP. Buildings constructed in a flood plain after a community has met regulations must conform to elevation requirements. About 20,000 communities participate in the program. When repair, reconstruction or improvement to an older building equals or exceeds 50 percent of its market value, the structure must be updated to conform to current building codes. Older buildings sustain six times more damage than newer, elevated buildings built to flood-plains management standards, according to the Federal Insurance Administration. According to a 2007 NFIP study on the benefits of elevating buildings, homeowners can recover the higher construction costs in less than five years if the home is being built in a velocity zone where the structure is likely to be subject to wave damage, and in five to 15 years in a standard flood zone, through significantly lower insurance premiums.

Legislation was enacted in 1994 to tighten enforcement of flood insurance requirements. Regulators can now fine banks with a pattern of failure to enforce the law and lenders can purchase flood insurance on behalf of homeowners who fail to buy it themselves, then bill them for coverage. The law includes a provision that denies federal disaster aid to people who have been flooded twice and have failed to purchase insurance after the first flood. Another provision allows homeowners the option of purchasing flood mitigation insurance, coverage similar in concept to an ordinance or law endorsement, to help pay the cost of raising a structure above flood level to meet federal flood requirements.

Flood insurance was initially only available through insurance agents who dealt with a firm under contract with the Federal Insurance Administration (FIA), part of the Federal Emergency Management Agency (FEMA), to provide administrative services and maintain records. The "direct" policy program has been supplemented since 1983 with a program known as "Write Your Own," through which some 85 insurance companies issue policies and adjust flood claims on behalf of the federal government under their own names. The insurers receive a commission and remit premium income in excess of claims to the federal government. The FIA pays losses in excess of premiums; sets the rates, coverage limitations and eligibility requirements; and designates flood plain areas. The NFIP is expected to be self-supporting (i.e., premiums are set at an actuarially sound level) in an average loss year, as reflected in past experience. In an extraordinary year, as Hurricane Katrina demonstrated, losses can greatly exceed premiums. Hurricane Katrina losses and the percentage of flood damage that was uninsured have led to calls for a revamping of the entire flood program.

Flood plain maps are redrawn periodically. As development in and around flood plains increases, run-off patterns change, causing flooding in areas that were formerly not considered high risk. In addition, new technology enables flood mitigation programs to more accurately pinpoint areas vulnerable to flooding. Since the inception of the federal program, some 25 to 30 percent of all paid losses were for damage in areas not officially designated at the time of loss as flood-prone. A new report published by FEMA in 2007 suggests that development patterns should be changed to protect environmentally sensitive areas and that communities in the flood program should be encouraged or required to ban development in these locations.

Flood insurance covers direct physical losses by flood and losses resulting from flood-related erosion caused by waves or currents of water exceeding anticipated cyclical levels and accompanied by a severe storm, flash flood, abnormal tide surge or a similar situation which results in flooding. Buildings are covered for replacement cost but coverage for personal possessions is available on an actual cash value basis only. Coverage for the contents of basements is limited. To prevent people putting off the purchase of coverage until waters are rising and flooding is inevitable, policy-holders now have to wait 30 days before their policy takes effect. In 1993, 7,800 policies purchased at the last minute resulted in $48 million in claims against only $625,000 in premiums.

More than 11 million U.S. homes are in flood zones. Only about one in four homeowners who live in areas vulnerable to floods purchase federal flood insurance from the NFIP, generally those in the highest risk areas, in part because people underestimate the risk of flood damage. They tend to think the risk of flooding for structures in a flood zone is about the same as the risk of fire, when in fact it is much higher. According to a FEMA probability analysis, over the life of a 30 year mortgage, a property located in a special flood hazard area would have a 26 percent chance of being flooded, compared with a 1 percent chance of suffering a fire loss.

## Effect of Natural Disaster on Insurance Market

In conventional insurance markets the insurer faces a large number of independent risks that tend to follow a fairly predictable pattern across time. By charging premiums that the firm can invest and earn a return on before paying off the losses, the firm will be able to run a profitable insurance business.

Catastrophic losses caused by natural disasters are much more problematic from an insurance standpoint. Rather than a large number of risks that on average follow a quite predictable year-to-year pattern, catastrophic losses tend to be lumpy. In fact, the situation parallels that Catastrophic risks consequently pose a variety of problems for insurers. First, because the losses arise from a small number of lumpy events, the insurer may not have sufficient resources to cover the losses. Less dramatically, the firm may suffer losses well in excess of the value of the premiums that it charged for the coverage. In the absence of adequate reinsurance, the firm may go bankrupt or may choose to exit a state in which there is a substantial exposure to such catastrophic risks. In response to losses incurred following Hurricane Katrina, which accounted for over $38 billion in insured losses last year, one major insurer, All state, has exited several coastal states while another, State Farm, has chosen not to renew some policies in these areas. The fourth-largest personal insurer in Florida, Poe Financial, went bankrupt.

The second ramification of catastrophic losses is that they will influence the rate structure even for firms that remain quite viable in the presence of natural disasters. Suppose that an insurer is writing coverage in a very high-risk state that experiences a major disaster once every decade. In that disaster year, the firm will suffer losses well in excess of premiums. For it to be profitable for the insurer to write coverage in the state, it will consequently have to charge more for insurance in the other years in which there are no catastrophes than it would if there were not the threat of catastrophic risks. Thus, one would expect to observe very high loss ratios in the catastrophic risk states in years in which a catastrophe has occurred and expect especially low loss ratios in the non-catastrophe years as compared to the loss ratios in states not subject to such catastrophic risks.

A third phenomenon linked to natural disasters is that of learning about the risks over time. The distribution of losses due to catastrophes may change over time for a variety of reasons. Locational patterns may have shifted over time, as reflected in increased construction in high-risk beachfront locales. There also may be shifts in weather patterns, as evidenced in the recent speculation that catastrophic losses from Hurricane Katrina are likely to increase in the presence of global warming. The hurricane season in the period 1995-2005 averaged 15 named storms per year, up from an average of 8.5 named storms from 19711994. To the extent that insurers are rational Bayesian decision makers, one would expect them to update their risk beliefs over time when writing insurance coverage. Somewhat surprisingly, there is no econometric analysis whatsoever that addresses these and other fundamental aspects of how catastrophic risks affect insurance markets. There have, of course, been extensive discussions of a conceptual nature as well as analyses of the potential role of reinsurance, but there has been no empirical examination of how catastrophic risks affect insurance company behaviour.

## Insurance Market Consequences of Catastrophes: Loss Ratios, Premiums and Losses

To explore the effects of catastrophic risks, *Born and Viscusi (2006)* explored the effects of catastrophic risks through a series of regression analyses of the effect of these various explanatory variables on loss ratios, premiums, and losses.

The database used by *Born and Viscusi (2006)* comprises of the state-level homeowners' insurance operations for all U.S. insurers from 1984 to 2004. They obtained the direct premiums earned and losses incurred statistics from the State Pages of insurers' annual filings with the National Association of Insurance Commissioners for all insurers with positive premiums in the homeowners' line. This dataset is also the source of our information on total premiums earned in a state, organizational form, and the number of states in which the insurer writes homeowners' coverage.

The number of firm-state units in the dataset declines steadily through the time period analyzed. Whereas there were 9,644 observations in 1984, by 2004 there were only 6,596 firm-state units in the dataset. The number of unique firms in the sample ranges from a high of 1,103 in 1990 to a low of 961 in 2004. These figures suggest that firms offering homeowners' coverage have consolidated their operations, electing to provide coverage in fewer and fewer states over time, but not exiting the U.S. market. The analysis links an insurer's state-level homeowners' experience to catastrophic events in the state. The compilation of catastrophic events at the state level revealed that some states are affected by catastrophes on a regular basis. Anticipated catastrophic events would be reflected in premiums if insurers are rational. Likewise, insurer underwriting performance should not be adversely affected by catastrophic events that are anticipated, but would be adversely affected by a greater-than-anticipated number of events, and enhanced by a lower than-anticipated number of events. To capture this relationship, Born and Viscusi (2006) created a variable by year and by state called Unexpected Catastrophes. This variable is defined as the difference between the number of actual catastrophic events in a given year and the average number of catastrophic events in that state over the 1984-2004 period. The second set of catastrophic variables used are what Born and Viscusi (2006) call Blockbuster Catastrophes. This variable is the number of blockbuster catastrophe events from Table 6 that occurred in that state in that particular year. While all catastrophic events were counted equally in the creation of the Unexpected Catastrophes variable, we expect that these blockbuster catastrophes may have a differential effect. Because these events have a more profound effect on insurers' performance, this variable equals the number of blockbuster catastrophic events in the state in which the insurer operates for a given year.

The next set of variables pertains to organizational form. Born and Viscusi (2006) used separate variables to distinguish whether the firm had a Mutual insurance structure, a Lloyd's insurance structure, or was a Reciprocal firm. The omitted category is that of stock firms. They also included four variables that reflect the overall size of the insurance companies' operations. The three national measures are the Number of States in which the insurer operates, the Total Homeowners' Premiums written by the insurance company throughout the country, and the Total National Premiums written by the insurance company in all lines of insurance. They included Total Premiums in State as a measure of the scale of the firm's operations within the state. One would expect smaller firms to be more susceptible to shocks than larger firms. Moreover, one would expect firms with a substantial presence in the state to be more reluctant to leave the state after a catastrophic event because of the losses associated with other lines. The final variable they included is a 1 variable for Restrictive Rate Regulation. In these states, the firm must obtain prior approval before changing its homeowners' insurance rates. A more restrictive state regulatory regime is expected to hinder an insurer's ability to recover financially following a catastrophic event.

A major concern in the literature on insurance is how premiums are adjusted over time in response to fluctuations in interest rates. This phenomenon, which is known in the literature as the underwriting cycle, is often captured in empirical analyses of insurance markets by including some type of interest rate variable. The subsequent regression analysis will be more general, in that Born and Viscusi (2006) include time-specific indicator variables for each year in the sample, thus sweeping out all time-dependent influences such as interest rate fluctuations and temporal trends in the number of firms writing homeowners insurance, as well as any other temporal effects.

## The Dependent Variables

### *(i) The Loss Ratio*

It is the ratio of losses incurred divided by premiums earned. The inverse of the loss ratio is the most widely accepted measure of insurance company profitability. Our hypothesis is that insurers that experience these catastrophic losses and blockbuster events will adjust their pricing practices so that the insurance they write in the years in which catastrophic events do not occur will be more profitable than insurance written in states not subject to a large number of catastrophes. This additional profitability is needed to compensate for the increased losses that these firms experience during the years in which major catastrophes occur.

Table 6 presents the regression of the natural logarithm of loss ratio on the series of explanatory variables. Specifically, we estimate:

$$\text{Loss Ratio}_{ist} = \alpha_1 + \beta_1 \text{ UnexpCat}_{ist} + \beta_2\text{UnexpCat}_{is,t-1} + \beta_3 \text{ UnexpCat}_{is,t-2} + \beta_4 \text{ Blockbuster}_{ist} + \beta_5 \text{ Blockbuster}_{is,t-1} + \beta_6 \text{ Blockbuster}_{is,t-2} + \beta_7 \text{ Mutual}_i + \beta_8 \text{ Lloyd'si} + \beta_9 \text{ Reciprocal}_i + \beta_{10} \text{ LnNumstsi t} + \beta_{11} \text{ LnHOPrems}_{i\,t} + \beta_{12} \text{ LnStatePrems}_{ist} + \beta_{13} \text{ LnNatPrems}_{it} + \beta_{14} \text{ RateRegis}_t + \Sigma \text{Yi} + \varepsilon_{1t} \quad (1)$$

for firm i in state s at time t, and where $Y_j$ is a dummy variable for each year j = 1985-2004. The main hypotheses are that unexpected catastrophes and blockbuster catastrophes should substantially boost the loss ratios that firms experience in the catastrophe years and lower loss ratios in the non-catastrophe years.

This basic set of predictions is in fact borne out in the results in Table 6. There is the expected positive effect of the current value of the catastrophe variable as well as the value lagged one year. Notably, two years after the unexpected catastrophe, there is a negative effect that is roughly the same size as the estimated standard error. Thus, the Unexpected Catastrophe variable lagged two years is consistent with the pricing hypothesis, but there is no statistically significant evidence of such

## Table 6
## Insurer Loss Ratio Regressions

| *Explanatory variable* | *Coefficient (Std. error)* |
|---|---|
| Intercept | -0.910 |
| | (0.043) |
| Unexpected Catastrophes t | 0.060 |
| | (0.002) |
| Unexpected Catastrophes t-1 | 0.019*** |
| | (0.002) |
| Unexpected Catastrophes t-2 | 0.002 |
| | (0.002) |
| Blockbuster Catastrophes t | 0.120*** |
| | (0.008) |
| Blockbuster Catastrophes t-1 | 0.004 |
| | (0.011) |
| Blockbuster Catastrophes t-2 | -0.085 |
| | (0.012) |
| Mutual | 0.019 |
| | (0.008) |
| Lloyd's | -0.038 |
| | (0.043) |
| Reciprocal | 0.115*** |
| | (0.019) |
| Ln (No. of States in which insurer operates) | -0.075*** |
| | (0.005) |
| Ln (Homeowners Premiums) | -0.015*** |
| | (0.002) |
| Ln (Total Premium in State) | 0.051*** |
| | (0.003) |
| Ln (Total National Premiums) | -0.005* |
| | (0.003) |
| Restrictive Rate Regulations | 0.034.*** |
| | (0.007) |
| Adjusted $R^2$ | 0.031 |

Regression includes 20 year dummies, which are not shown.

# Dependent variable = Ln (Loss Ratio).

*, ** and *** denote significance at the 90%, 95% and 99% level, two-tailed test.

*Source* : Patricia Born and W. Kip Viscusi (2006): The catastrophic effects of natural disasters on insurance markets, *Journal of Risk and Uncertainty* (2006), 33:5572.

an effect. The subsequent loss ratio offset is more pronounced for blockbuster catastrophes. The effect of blockbuster catastrophes is to boost the loss ratio during the year of the blockbuster catastrophe, but there is an opposite and almost offsetting effect two years later. This result is consistent with our hypothesis that after a blockbuster event, firms will raise their insurance premiums in order to provide sufficient coverage in case of future blockbuster catastrophes. These premium adjustments lead to lower future loss ratios during the years in which a blockbuster catastrophe does not strike. The evidence for such adjustments is much stronger for blockbuster catastrophes than for catastrophes more generally.

### *(ii) Premiums*

Table 7 presents the regression of the log of premiums earned against our set of explanatory variables. Specifically,

$$\text{LnHOPremsi}_{st} = \alpha_1 + \beta_1\text{LnHOPrems}_{is,t-1} + \beta_2\text{UnexpCat}_{ist} + \beta_3\text{UnexpCat}_{is,t-1} + \beta_4\text{UnexpCat}_{is,t-2} + \beta_5\ \text{Blockbuster}_{ist} + \beta_6\text{Blockbuster}_{is,t-1} + \beta_7\text{Blockbuster}_{is,t-2} + \beta 8\ \text{Mutual}_i + \beta_9\text{Lloyd'si} + \beta_{10}\text{Reciprocal}_i + \beta_{11}\text{LnNumsts}_{i\,t} + \beta_{12}\text{RateRegst} + \beta_{13}\text{LnStatePremsist} + \beta_{14}\text{LnNatPrems}_{i\,t} + \Sigma\ \delta\ jYj + \varepsilon_{ist}. \quad (2)$$

Premiums reflect both the price of insurance as well as the quantity of insurance, so in many respects are a less instructive measure than the loss ratio, which serves as an ex-post measure of insurer profitability.We include a measure of the one-period-lagged homeowners' premiums in the analysis as well to capture the fact that there is a strong autoregressive character to insurance underwriting, as firms that write a large number of premiums in the state in a given year will tend to continue to do so in subsequent years. Indeed, the elasticity of premiums earned to homeowners' premiums earned in the previous year is 0.973. Catastrophic events have a mixed effect on insurance premiums. One would expect these unexpected catastrophes or blockbuster events to raise the rate that firms charge for insurance. Thus, for any given number of policies written, the total premiums will rise. However, these major catastrophes also may reduce the quantity of insurance written, both because of the higher rates and insurance rationing, as well as exiting of firms from the state. The regression results in Table 7 indicate that the negative quantity effect is dominant. Unexpected catastrophes have a negative effect on premiums earned, both in the year of the catastrophe as well as in the subsequent year. Similarly, the blockbuster catastrophes are influential as well with a significant negative effect both in the current year as well as two years after the catastrophic event.

### *(iii) Losses*

The most easily predictable results are those pertaining to losses incurred. These major catastrophes should clearly boost the losses incurred

**TABLE 7**
**Regression Results for Insurer Premiums**

| *Explanatory variable* | *Coefficient (Std. error)* |
|---|---|
| Intercept | -0.976*** (0.035) |
| Ln (Homeowners Premiums)t-1 | 0.973*** (0.001) |
| Unexpected Catastrophes t | -0.027*** (0.002) |
| Unexpected Catastrophes t-1 | -0.022*** (0.002) |
| Unexpected Catastrophes t-2 | -0.023*** (0.002) |
| Blockbuster Catastrophes t | -0.033*** (0.007) |
| Blockbuster Catastrophes t-1 | 0.013 (0.009) |
| Blockbuster Catastrophes t-2 | -0.029*** (0.010) |
| Mutual | 0.156*** (0.007) |
| Lloyd's | 0.241*** (0.037) |
| Reciprocal | 0.225*** (0.017) |
| Ln (No of States in which insurer operates) | 0.088*** (0.004) |
| Restrictive Rate Regulation | -0.015*** (0.006) |
| Ln (Total Premium in State) | 0.109*** (0.002) |
| Ln (Total National Premiums) | -0.041*** (0.003) |
| Adjusted $R^2$ | 0.896 |

*Note* : Regression includes 20 year dummies, which are not shown.

# Dependent variable = Ln (Premiums Earned).

*, **and *** denote significance at the 90%, 95% and 99% level, two-tailed test.

*Source* : Patricia Born and W. Kip Viscusi (2006): The catastrophic effects of natural disasters on insurance markets, *Journal of Risk and Uncertainty,* (2006) 33:5572.

by the insurance company, controlling for the scale of the company's operations ( this is done by including the lagged value of the homeowners' premiums written by the company in that state). Thus Born and Viscusi (2006) estimate:

$$LnHOLosses_{ist} = \alpha_1 + \beta_1 LnHOPrems_{is,t-1} + \beta_2 UnexpCat_{ist} + \beta_3 UnexpCat_{is,t-1} + \beta_4 UnexpCat_{is,t-2} + \beta_5 Blockbusterist + \beta_6 Blockbuster_{is,t-1} + \beta_7 Blockbuster_{is,t-2} + \beta_8 Mutual_i + \beta_9 Lloyd's_i + \beta_{10} Reciprocal_i + \beta_{11} LnNumsts_{it} + \beta_{12} RateReg_{ist} + \beta_{13} LnStatePrems_{ist} + \beta_{14} LnNatPrems_{it} + \Sigma\delta_j Y_i + \varepsilon_{ist} \quad (3)$$

The results, shown in Table 8, suggest that unexpected catastrophes raise the value of losses incurred, both in the year of the catastrophe as well as in the subsequent year. About three-fourths of the influence occurs in the current year, with the remainder occurring with a one-period lag. Blockbuster catastrophes raise the value of losses in the year of the catastrophe, but two years later reduce the value of losses. This effect of reducing losses two years after a catastrophe would be expected, to the extent that the blockbuster event leads to either a reduced quantity of insurance written or the exit of the firm from the state insurance market altogether.

TABLE 8

**Regression Results : Effect of Unexpected Catastrophic Events on Insurer Losses**

| *Explanatory variable* | *Coefficient (Std. error)* |
|---|---|
| Intercept | -0.910<br>(0.043) |
| Ln (Homeowners Premiums) t-1 | 0.985***<br>(0.002) |
| Unexpected Catastrophes t | 0.060***<br>(0.002) |
| Unexpected Catastrophes t-1 | 0.019***<br>(0.002) |
| Unexpected Catastrophes t-2 | -0.002<br>(0.002) |
| Blockbuster Catastrophes t | 0.120***<br>(0.008) |
| Blockbuster Catastrophes t-1 | 0.004<br>(0.011) |
| Blockbuster Catastrophes t-2 | -0.085***<br>(0.012) |

| | |
|---|---|
| Mutual | 0.019*** |
| | (0.008) |
| Lloyd's | -0.038 |
| | (0.043) |
| Reciprocal | 0.115*** |
| | (0.019) |
| Ln (No. of states in which insurer operates) | -0.075*** |
| | (0.005) |
| Restrictive Rate Regulation | 0.034*** |
| | (0.007) |
| Ln (Total Premiums in State) | 0.051 |
| | (0.003) |
| Ln (Total National Premiums) | -0.005* |
| | (0.003) |
| Adjusted $R^2$ | 0.850 |

Regression includes 20 year dummies, which are not shown.
#Dependent variable = Ln (Losses Incurred).
*, ** and ***denote significance at the 90%, 95% and 99% level, two-tailed test.

*Source* : Patricia Born and W. Kip Viscusi (2006): The catastrophic effects of natural disasters on insurance markets, *Journal of Risk and Uncertainty,* (2006) 33:557.

## Natural Disaster Management: The Indian Scenario

In India, the Central Government acts as an *ex post* insurer. That is, it provides assistance after an incident occurs.The current funding system has 2 components:

[a] The CRF i.e. the Calamity Relief Fund and [b] the NCCF i.e. the National Calamity Contingency Fund.

### *[a] The Calamity Relief Fund*

The CRF is meant to be used for immediate relief and rescue operations. It is allocated state wise every 5 years by the Finance Commission. There is also a yearly allocation made to individual states on the basis of the state public expenditure. For the period 2001-05, the Finance Commission has allocated roughly Rs. 10,000 crores for the CRF. Of this, the states contribute 25% and the center, 75%. Currently, the amount remaining at the end of 5 years can be used by the states for planned expenditure.

### *[b] The National Calamity Contingency Fund*

The Tenth Finance Commission for the first time formulated a distinct funding mechanism for taking care of calamities of rare severity. The

TABLE 9
**Release of Assistance from NCCF (2000-01 to 2004-05)**

*(Figures in Rs. Crores)*

| *State* | *2000-01* | *2001-02* | *2002-03* | *2003-04* | *2004-05* | *Total* |
|---|---|---|---|---|---|---|
| Andhra Pradesh | 0.00 | 30.44 | 59.94 | 116.75 | 87.20 | 294.33 |
| Arunachal Pradesh | 2.00 | 0.00 | 12.78 | 29.79 | 9.09 | 53.66 |
| Assam | 0.00 | 0.00 | 0.00 | 0.00 | 211.55 | 211.55 |
| Bihar | 29.67 | 0.00 | 0.00 | 0.00 | 398.92 | 428.59 |
| Chhattisgarh | 40.00 | 42.88 | 100.68 | 26.83 | 52.74 | 263.13 |
| Goa | 0.00 | 0.00 | 0.00 | 0.00 | 0.00 | 0.00 |
| Gujarat | 585.00 | 994.37 | 23.29 | 32.41 | 55.00 | 1690.07 |
| Haryana | 0.00 | 0.00 | 0.00 | 2.20 | 0.00 | 2.20 |
| Himachal Pradesh | 8.29 | 61.48 | 14.05 | 0.30 | 0.00 | 84.12 |
| Jammu & Kashmir | 0.00 | 23.20 | 0.00 | 0.00 | 50.00 | 73.20 |
| Jharkhand | 0.00 | 0.00 | 0.00 | 0.00 | 0.00 | 0.00 |
| Karnataka | 0.00 | 0.00 | 196.88 | 316.47 | 63.62 | 576.97 |
| Kerala | 0.00 | 0.00 | 0.00 | 0.00 | 206.00 | 206.00 |
| Madhya Pradesh | 35.00 | 22.72 | 183.34 | 36.72 | 1.70 | 279.48 |
| Maharashtra | 0.00 | 0.00 | 20.00 | 77.46 | 173.23 | 270.69 |
| Manipur | 0.00 | 0.00 | 7.07 | 0.00 | 0.00 | 7.07 |
| Meghalaya | 1.00 | 0.00 | 0.00 | 0.00 | 6.16 | 7.16 |
| Mizoram | 0.00 | 0.00 | 0.00 | 0.00 | 10.68 | 10.68 |
| Nagaland | 0.00 | 0.00 | 0.00 | 0.00 | 1.81 | 1.81 |
| Orissa | 35.00 | 114.62 | 21.84 | 104.43 | 53.44 | 329.33 |
| Punjab | 0.00 | 0.00 | 0.00 | 0.00 | 0.00 | 0.00 |
| Rajasthan | 85.00 | 78.97 | 434.08 | 512.74 | 216.79 | 1327.58 |
| Sikkim | 0.00 | 0.00 | 0.00 | 0.00 | 9.90 | 9.90 |
| Tamilnadu | 0.00 | 0.00 | 215.99 | 289.45 | 783.14 | 1288.58 |
| Tripura | 0.00 | 0.00 | 0.00 | 0.00 | 0.05 | 0.05 |
| Uttar Pradesh | 0.00 | 0.00 | 310.06 | 41.87 | 192.10 | 544.03 |
| Uttaranchal | 0.00 | 0.00 | 0.00 | 0.00 | 0.00 | 0.00 |
| West Bengal | 103.25 | 0.00 | 0.00 | 0.00 | 0.00 | 103.25 |
| Total | 924.21 | 1368.68 | 1600.00 | 1587.42 | 2583.12 | 8063.43 |

*Source* : www.finmin.nic.in

Commission recommended setting up of a "National Fund for Calamity Relief" (NFCR) with a corpus of Rs. 700 crore to be constituted by the Centre and the States in the ratio of 75:25 over a period of 5 years.The Eleventh Finance Commission changed its format and renamed it as National Calamity Contingency Fund. The Government of India contributed an initial core amount of Rs. 500 crore to this fund, to be replenished by the levy of the special surcharge as and when any drawls are made from it. The Twelfth Finance Commission recommended continuation of the scheme in its present form with core corpus of Rs. 500 crores.

The NCCF covers natural calamities of cyclone, drought, earthquake, fire, flood, tsunami, hailstorm, landslide, avalanche, cloud burst and pest attack. The procedure of release of resources from NCCF is as under:

> Consequent on the receipt of memorandum from the State Government, a Central Team is deputed for making on the spot assessment. Report of the Central Team is examined by an Inter-Ministerial Group (IMG). IMG recommendations are considered by High Level Committee (HLC) consisting of Agricultural Minister, Home Minister, Finance Minister and Deputy Chairman, Planning Commission. HLC decides about the quantum of assistance and release of funds from NCCF. Releases to the States under NCCF are made by the Finance Commission Division. State-wise releases from NCCF for the period 2000-01 to 2004-05 are as under.

## Section VI

## MANAGING THE IMPACT OF NATURAL DISASTER—THE IMPORTANT ISSUES

To some extent, countries can prepare themselves for natural disaster by adapting their physical environment and their economies and by purchasing insurance. In its 2001 World Disaster Report, the Red cross argued that investments of $40 billion in disaster preparedness, prevention, and mitigation would have reduced global economic losses in the 1990s by $280 billion.

### (a) Preventive Measures

Planning for natural disaster has a set of common tools employed in the developed world. The first tools deal with the reduction of risk prior to an event occurring. These tools are generally classified as mitigation activity, and are directed at either reducing exposure to natural disaster events or increasing the ability of structures to withstand the impact of the natural disasters. As such, developed countries have done much more than developing countries to protect themselves against natural disasters. The

United States, in particular, significantly increased expenditures on preparedness, mitigation, and recovery during the disaster-prone 1990s—$1.9 billion in fiscal 1999 alone, according to the National Emergency Management Association. In contrast, many developing countries lack the financial resources, technical knowledge, and political will to mitigate physical vulnerability. Moreover, in many countries—especially the small island countries—physical adaptation is inordinately expensive. And mitigation measures can eliminate only some of the risk, much of which stems from the movement of people to disaster-prone areas.

### *(i) Managing Climatic Change*

On a worldwide policy level, the causes of climatic change must be pursued. While the scientific links between human activity and increased global mean temperature continue to be explored, the international community must take into account increasing loss burdens for developing countries from natural disasters. This increasing burden is caused by the dual trends of increasing concentration of vulnerable assets in hazard prone regions, and the likelihood of increased severe natural atmospheric natural disasters.

### *(ii) Land Use Planning*

Land use planning attempts to reduce construction on seismic fault lines, coastal regions subject to windstorm or storm surge damage, and river shorelines subject to floods. While among the most effective of risk reduction measures, land use planning has proven to be difficult to implement (Kunreuther, 1998). Governments can also promote farming practices that enable farmers to weather climatic variations—using drought-resistant crop varieties, for instance—and help farmers increase their ability to adapt to long-term change. To ensure adequate water supply, governments may need to anticipate increased seasonal variation and greater frequency of both storms and dry periods.

### *(iii) Engineering/Ecological Measures*

Another strategy reduces risk through engineering or ecological measures. These approaches attempt to reduce the impact of natural disasters by some form of engineering or ecological intervention. The creation of dams for flood control, dikes to reroute flood waters, reforestation activity or seawalls to break storm surges are examples of this approach. An additional engineering approach reduces the impact of natural disasters on individual structures. The use of proper construction techniques can substantially reduce the loss of life from earthquakes and flooding. The use of these measures requires weighing the comparative cost of the mitigation measure with the benefits to be received.

## (b) Fiscal Preparation for Natural Disaster

Countries at risk must also prepare themselves fiscally for natural disasters. The risk of natural disaster creates a contingent liability of a particularly difficult kind, given the implicit guarantees given to—or at least perceived by—the private sector. Because of the lack of demand for, or unavailability of, insurance in many developing and emerging market countries, governments assume substantial risk for reconstruction after a disaster. (For example, the World Bank estimates that approximately 50 percent of its post-disaster funding goes to restore damaged housing.) More generally, the protection of those affected by disaster is widely seen as a basic duty of government. Countries must identify and acknowledge such contingent liabilities. This requires assessing the probabilities and costs of the various natural disasters that might befall them. Clearly, there is considerable uncertainty as to, for example, the maximum loss that might be suffered. There is, however, considerable historical information to build on. Combining this with evidence on current trends, a rough estimate should be feasible. A recent study by the World Bank, Swiss Re, and the International Institute for Applied Systems Analysis illustrates how natural disaster loss calculations can be integrated into the World Bank's macroeconomic planning model for countries. Some provisioning against the risk of disaster may also be appropriate. While governments typically set-up contingency funds to deal with unanticipated spending needs, natural disasters are not systematically factored into the calculations. A number of countries have been exploring the use of reserve funds for post-disaster financing. Mexico's FONDEN, for example, is an annual budgetary allocation for natural disaster expenditures. While it is evidently impossible to set aside enough to meet the costs of all conceivable disasters—and this would, in any event, not be the best use of scarce development funds—the importance of covering the immediate costs makes it prudent to adopt a fiscal stance that provides some degree of self-insurance. Disaster risk makes it appropriate for a government to adopt a tighter long-term fiscal stance (with possible exceptions for investment in measures of adaptation). In general, one would expect the amount set aside to be higher (relative to the expected loss) the larger the potential loss relative to national income, the greater the likelihood of disaster, the more expensive the insurance, and the more risk-averse the government. Governments, especially in developing countries, can also offset failures in local insurance markets—for example, by issuing guarantees to insurers and reinsurers (guarantees that might then be hedged in world reinsurance and capital markets). There may also be scope for simply requiring certain parties to buy at least a minimum amount of insurance coverage. Not least, governments might do more to insure their own property. The international financial institutions can support these efforts by tackling market failures and helping to finance relief and adaptation efforts. Prompt foreign assistance can reduce both the long-term macroeconomic damage caused by natural disasters—although some physical losses may be permanent (for example, irreversible soil erosion caused by severe flooding)—and the costs of recovery. The quicker output recovers, the less the public sector will need to borrow or monetize, and the sooner clean water is restored, the lower the morbidity impact.

### (c) Real Time Post-disaster Response

Another planning tool combines pre disaster planning with immediate post-disaster response. These activities fall within the general terminology of disaster emergency preparedness planning. The use of early warning system, evacuation of hazard prone regions, creation of temporary housing and life support systems, and other activities immediately around the disaster event are incorporated within this planning activity. This disaster planning activity can have a dramatic impact in reducing the lives lost and property damaged from natural disasters.

## *Natural Disaster : Risk Management*

During the past decade, scientific understanding of the causes and consequences of natural disasters has dramatically improved. Models to predict the frequency and severity of disaster events have been blended with sophisticated techniques to measure economic vulnerability to catastrophic losses. In the developed world, these models have been used extensively to evaluate potential exposure to natural disaster losses and expand the tools available to absorb these risks. (Kleindorfer and Kunreuther, 1999) This activity has not only increased the predictability of natural disasters, but also the ability to estimate potential consequences of these events.

The vulnerability of a community or region to natural disasters includes the potential for direct damage to residential, commercial and industrial property, other facilities such as schools, hospitals, and government buildings as well as infrastructure damage to highways, water, gas, electricity and other lifelines. Any disruption of infrastructure such as loss of the water supply or electric power can cause indirect losses by interrupting business activity, forcing families to evacuate their homes and causing emotional stress to families. One also has to consider the exposure of the population to the hazard and potential number of fatalities and injuries to different socioeconomic groups.

The ingredients for evaluating the vulnerability of a city or region to natural hazards are risk assessment and societal conditions. Ideally a *risk assessment* specifies the probability of events of different intensities or magnitudes occurring and the impact of the direct and indirect impacts of these events to the affected interested parties. *Societal conditions* include human settlement patterns, the built environment, day-to-day activities and the institutions established to deal with natural hazards.

Before developing a disaster management strategy one needs to understand the decision processes of the key stakeholders. The term decision processes refers to the type of information and data collected by individuals, groups and/or organizations (either private or public) and how they are utilized in making choices. For example, if a family is considering whether to bolt its home to a foundation to reduce future losses from a severe earthquake, what information does it collect on both the hazard itself and the potential damage with and without this mitigation measure? What type of decision rule(s) does the family utilize in determining whether or not to invest in this mitigation measure? What type of data and decision rules do firms utilize in evaluating the cost-effectiveness of different mitigation measure? How do the strategies of firms regarding adoption of mitigation measures relate to their profit objectives as well as their financial concerns should they suffer large losses

FIG. 7
**Framework for Analysis**

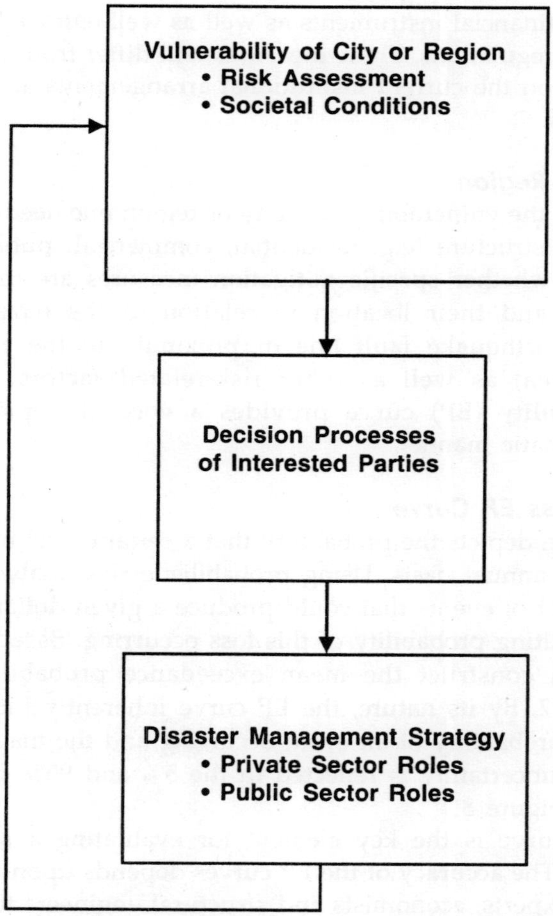


*Source* : Howard Kunreuther (2001): Mitigation and Financial Risk Management for Natural Hazards, Working Paper, The Wharton School, University of Pennsylvania.

from catastrophic events? What factors influence the public sector's decisions as to what regulations and standards they should issue relative to protection against the damage from natural disasters? What is the basis for their actions regarding the types of financial assistance provided to victims of these catastrophes?

Unless we understand the nature of the decision processes of these and other interested parties, it will be difficult recommending specific programs or policies that are likely to be implemented.

Based on an understanding of the vulnerability of the city or region and the decision processes of the key interested parties, one needs to develop a strategy for reducing losses and providing financial protection to victims of future disasters. This strategy will normally involve a combination of private and public sector initiatives which include insurance and new financial instruments as well as well-enforced building codes and land-use regulations. These measures will differ from country to country depending on the current institutional arrangements and existing legislation and laws.

### *Vulnerability of a Region*

In determining the vulnerability of a city or region one needs to know the design of each structure (e.g. residential, commercial, public sector) and infrastructure, whether specific mitigation measures are in place or could be utilized, and their location in relation to the hazard. (e.g., distance from an earthquake fault line or proximity to the coast in a hurricane-prone area) as well as other risk-related factors. The loss exceedance probability (EP) curve provides a way of depicting this damage in a systematic manner.

### *Constructing a Loss EP Curve*

A loss EP curve depicts the probability that a certain level of loss will be exceeded on an annual basis. Using probabilistic risk analysis (PRA), one combines the set of events that could produce a given dollar loss and determines the resulting probability of this loss occurring. Based on these estimates, one can construct the mean exceedance probability curve depicted in Figure 2. By its nature, the EP curve inherently incorporates uncertainty in the probability of an event occurring and the magnitude of dollar losses. This uncertainty is reflected in the 5% and 95% confidence interval curves in Figure 8.

The loss EP curve is the key element for evaluating a set of risk management tools. The accuracy of the EP curves depends upon the ability of natural hazard experts, economists and structural engineers to estimate the impact of events of different probabilities and magnitudes on the performance of different structures.

**FIG. 8**
**Example of Loss Exceedance Probability (EP) Curves**

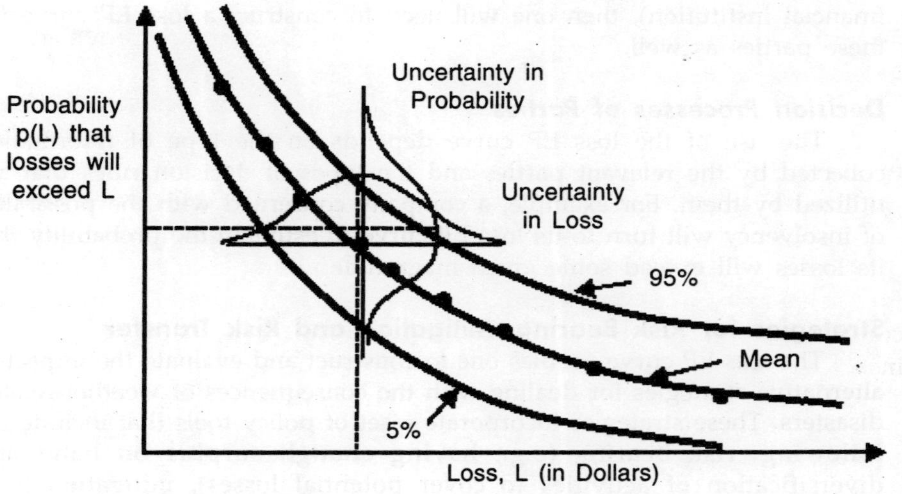


*Source* : Howard Kunreuther (2001): Mitigation and Financial Risk Management for Natural Hazards, Working Paper, The Wharton School, University of Pennsylvania.

### *The Loss EP Curve as an Integrating Concept*

The following elements are necessary if one is to construct a loss EP curve as an integrating concept for linking risk assessment with risk management strategies for reducing the vulnerability of a city or region.

### *Nature of the Problem*

To begin the analysis, it is important to specify the nature of the problem one is studying and to indicate why it is considered important. Normally, the problem of concern is a weather-related hazard where there is some likelihood (often small) that there will be a high impact event which produces severe economic consequences.

### *Characterizing the Risk*

One needs to rely on expert judgment to estimate the chances of certain events occurring and their potential consequences. In utilizing these estimates, it is valuable to have a notion of the degree of uncertainty surrounding these figures.

### *Parties Affected by the Risk*

One needs to specify the relevant parties affected by the risk. Suppose the analysis is being undertaken for a company who is concerned with potential losses from a weather-related hazard. Then the loss EP curve will depict the potential losses to the firm from a series of events, such as earthquakes of different magnitudes and intensities. If other stakeholders are involved in helping to cover these losses (*e.g.*, an insurer, reinsurer or financial institution), then one will need to construct a loss EP curve for these parties as well.

### *Decision Processes of Parties*

The use of the loss EP curve depends on the type of information collected by the relevant parties and the types of decision rules that are utilized by them. For example, a company concerned with the possibility of insolvency will turn to its loss EP curve to estimate the probability that its losses will exceed some given magnitude.

### Strategies for Risk Bearing, Mitigation and Risk Transfer

The loss EP curve enables one to construct and evaluate the impact of alternative strategies for dealing with the consequences of weather-related disasters. These strategies incorporate a set of policy tools that include the following: risk bearing (e.g., having enough surplus on hand and diversification of activities to cover potential losses), mitigation (e.g., investing in a measure to reduce future disaster losses), and risk transfer (e.g., use of insurance, reinsurance and catastrophe bonds to lay-off a portion of one's risk to others).

### Protection Against Catastrophic Losses : Behaviour of the Firm

The recent literature in economics suggests that firms are generally risk averse and hence are concerned with non-diversifiable risks such as catastrophic losses from natural disasters (Mayers and Smith, 1982). Suppose a firm is risk averse and there are transaction costs associated with bankruptcy. Then, the firm will want to purchase protection against catastrophic losses at higher premiums than implied by their expected losses, even when their shareholders can eliminate this risk through their own portfolio diversification. Firms are also likely to be ambiguity averse. In other words, they are concerned with the uncertainty regarding the probability of a loss occurring (Kunreuther, Hogarth and Meszaros, 1993).

### Importance of Safety—First Constraints and Shareholder Concerns

One way to reflect the firm's risk aversion and ambiguity aversion is a safety-first model first proposed by the French economist Roy (1952). Such a model can be contrasted with a value maximization approach to firm behaviour. A safety-first model explicitly concerns itself with insolvency when a firm makes a decision as to how much protection it would like to have against catastrophic losses and how much it is willing to pay to protect itself against this possibility. James Stone (1973) utilized a form of this safety-first model to characterize insurers' underwriting decisions. More specifically he postulated that the underwriter's objective is to charge a premium that maximizes the firm's expected profits subject to the following constraint: the probability of the claims from a disaster exceeding the insurer's total assets (i.e., the firm becomes insolvent) is less than some pre-specified value

Even with their concerns with insolvency, firms need to determine how they can satisfy their shareholders concerns that they receive a positive return on assets (ROA) in any given year. An insurance company could increase its ROA by raising the selling price of its policies, thereby collecting more premiums. However, if it increased this premium rate too much, the demand for insurance would fall, limiting the number of policies the insurer could write. Hence, an insurer must meet its safety-first constraint while maximizing return on assets and assuring sufficient demand. Demand for insurance is not only a function of the premium rate, but also of policy features such as deductible level and insurance cap. For example, if an insurer is currently writing policies with 10% deductibles, a policy-holder will be responsible for any losses up to 10% of the value of his home. If his home is worth Rs. 10,00,000, the insurer will not pay for any damages less than Rs. 100,000. The insurer covers all losses greater than this level. If the insurer raises the deductible to 20%, the policy-holder will now be responsible for twice as much loss, or damages up to Rs. 200,000. As the deductible increases, the policy-holder's demand for insurance falls.

Suppose the insurer instead wrote policies with no deductible but instated an insurance cap of Rs. 5,00,000 on the maximum insured value per structure. Now the policyholder is responsible for losses between Rs. 5,00,000 and Rs. 10,00,000 (the value of the structure). If the insurer lowers the insurance cap to Rs. 400,000, the policy-holder is now responsible for losses between Rs. 400,000 and Rs. 10,00,000. A reduction in the level of insurance cap will decrease demand for insurance as long as the cap is low enough to affect policyholders. Insurers must guarantee that there is adequate demand for their policies. Consequently, they must monitor the premium rate, the deductible level and the insurance cap level.

## Developing Risk Management Strategies to Satisfy Conflicting Objectives

The safety-first model and profit/value maximization approach can be used together in evaluating risk management strategies. Due to the cost of the risk transfer instrument and the reduction in premiums collected, a downward shift in the loss distribution in order to meet a safety-first constraint will result in a lower return on assets for a fixed percentage book of business. The tradeoffs between the safety-first and return on assets can make some books of business infeasible even if mitigation or risk transfer mechanisms are used. For example, suppose purchasing a catastrophe bond reduces an insurer's insolvency probability below the target level, but brings about a negative return on assets. This catastrophe bond strategy is infeasible because the insurance company's shareholders require a positive return on assets. If the insurer is not able to net a positive return on assets with any strategy, the risk is not insurable.

We assume that a typical insurer is decentralized and has little control over the number of policies its agents sell. Thus, the number of policies written is independent of the insurer's particular risk management strategy. For example, the insurer's decision to issue a catastrophe bond or selectively underwrite should not affect the number of policies agents sell if the premiums remain the same. Most of the analyses below fix the number of policies written under all strategies at an arbitrary level.

A firm concerned with managing catastrophe risk is likely to have a series of low probability high consequence (lp-hc) events in its loss distribution. High consequence events are those that threaten the solvency of a firm. In other words, the magnitude of loss from the lp-hc event is greater than the firm's surplus. These lp-hc events show up as an elongated right tail in the graph of the Loss EP curve. For example, due to the catastrophic potential of earthquakes in Northern California, an insurance company with a randomly selected book of business in Oakland is likely to face significant lp-hc events.

Suppose the surplus of the firm (i.e. the initial assets plus the total premiums collected) is greater than the loss on the EP curve corresponding to the target insolvency probability EP(LTR)= β*, where β* is the target insolvency probability and LTR is the corresponding target ruin loss). Then the safety-first constraint is satisfied and a reasonable level of solvency is guaranteed. For example, if â* = .01 and LTR = $1 million, then the firm requires that its surplus be greater than $1 million. More generally, the safety-first constraint can be expressed as:

Probability (Surplus $\leq$ LTR) β*
where Surplus = Initial Assets + Total Premiums Collected

LTR increases with increases in the magnitude of lp-hc losses and the firm is less likely to meet the safety-first constraint. For example, if the insurer changes its strategy by only insuring in a highhazard earthquake area of Oakland rather than in lower risk areas of the city and continues to write the same number of policies as before, then for β* = .01 its LTR might increase from $1 million to $ 2 million. Given the nature of the safety-first constraints in industries like insurance, even firms with minimal catastrophe loss exposure are likely to face some difficulty in meeting the target insolvency probability on randomly selected books of business.

A profit, or value maximization model mandates that firms optimize their returns on investment, making expensive risk reduction and risk transfer instruments less attractive because they significantly reduce the return on assets. If firms operate in competitive environments where demand is elastic, they cannot increase the price of their product (i.e. raise the total amount of premiums collected) without reducing demand. Consequently, firms must actively choose a book of business that has a relatively low exposure to lp-hc events. At this point, risk reduction and risk transfer mechanisms may prove effective in managing the tradeoffs of the constraints. In summary, it is important to understand that the feasibility of a particular risk management strategy depends on the nature and specifications of the constraints. Therefore, one must carefully select appropriate constraints and their related parameters (e.g. $\beta^*$, LTR).

## Strategies for Reducing Insurer Losses

One way to reduce the chances of insolvency is to shift the EP curve downward so that the chances of catastrophic losses are reduced to an acceptable risk level. In addition insurers can utilize risk transfer mechanisms to shift their catastrophic losses to another party, such as a reinsurer or investor in catastrophic bonds.

## Underwriting and Mitigation Strategies

An insurer can institute a variety of underwriting decision rules, each of which will have different effects on the shape of the Loss EP curve. Some strategies shift the entire curve to lower loss levels, reducing catastrophic losses as well as expected losses and hence premiums. The ideal strategy would reduce the losses in the right tail, and keep the losses in the left tail fixed. This way, the insurer can continue to charge similar premiums since the expected loss has not fallen by a large amount, and will still see improvements in the probability of insolvency. One approach would be to raise deductible levels so that the payouts from any disaster would decrease. Another alternative would involve setting a cap on the maximum insured value of each structure in its book of business. A deductible has an impact on losses from disasters of any magnitude. An insurance cap, on the other hand, affects claims when there are large losses to individuals by placing a limit on the maximum claims payment to the homeowner. If homeowners, like insurers, wish to manage their exposure to catastrophes, they would prefer a deductible to an insurance cap. Although a low value for the insurance cap reduces the losses to the insurer, it is likely to be met with decreased demand for insurance.

Selective underwriting strategies can further reduce the insurer's insolvency probability. The firm can selectively choose which risks to include in issuing policies rather than insuring a randomly selected book of business from high-hazard areas. For example, the insurer's central office can instruct its agents only to sell policies to homeowners whose structure values fall in a predetermined range such as those less than $150,000. This particular underwriting rule effectively creates a cap on possible losses by limiting policies to less expensive homes. Alternatively, the central office can restrict its agents to selling policies in certain geographic areas.

Another way for insurers to reduce its insolvency probability would be to adopt loss reduction (mitigation) measures. In essence, the mitigation measure shifts the EP curve downward to reflect the lower probability of losses from the case when no loss reduction measures were in place. For instance, if a building code is instituted in an area, requiring homeowners to take mitigation measures, all insurers benefit from the reduction in the EP curve. If no regulations are in place, the insurer can selectively issue policies only on mitigated structures. Loss reduction measures reduce the chance of the firm becoming insolvent, making the safety-first constraint easier to meet.

### Risk Transfer Mechanisms

Risk transfer mechanisms complement underwriting strategies and mitigation measures by enabling an insurer to survive financially should its suffer a catastrophic loss. More specifically, the firm would use its EP curve to determine how much protection it would need to reduce its probability of insolvency below the target ruin probability â*. The more risk averse the firm is, the more it will need to use risk transfer instruments to protect itself against large losses, and the more it is willing to pay for this protection. Like mitigation, risk transfer instruments reduce the probability of insolvency. However, insurance companies pay premiums to purchase risk transfer instruments. Two risk transfer mechanisms are discussed below.

### Indemnity Contracts

Risk-averse firms may want to purchase an indemnity contract to cover losses above a certain amount. For a corporation, the normal indemnity contract is an insurance policy; for an insurer, the typical indemnity contract is an excess-of-loss reinsurance policy that provides coverage against unforeseen or extraordinary losses. A typical excess-of-loss reinsurance contract requires the primary insurer to retain a specified level of risk and then covers all losses between an attachment point (LA) and exhaustion point (*LE*) on the exceedance probability curve (Figure 9 ). In other words, the indemnity contract is of the following form: the reinsurer pays all losses in the interval *LA* to *LE* with a maximum payment of *LE-LA*. In return for this protection, the insurer pays the reinsurer a premium. A firm can significantly improve its risk exposure if it purchases an indemnity contract on its right tail (lp-hc) losses.

### Index-Based or Parameterized Contracts

As an alternative to an indemnity contract, a firm may want to utilize an index-based or parametric contract to obtain needed funds should a severe disaster occur. Today, a commonly utilized parametric contract is an indexed catastrophe linked bond (henceforth referred to as a *cat bond*). A cat bond requires the investor to give money up front that will be used by the firm if some type of triggering event occurs. In exchange for a high

FIG. 9

**Indemnity Contract and Loss EP Curve**

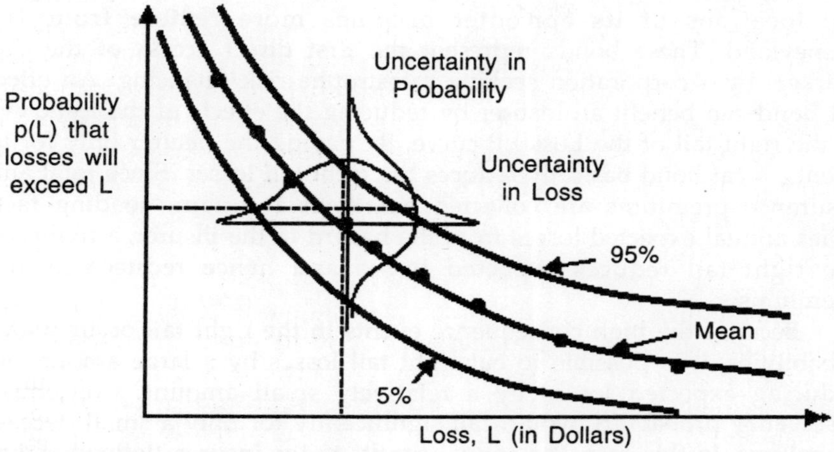


*Source* : Howard Kunreuther (2001): Mitigation and Financial Risk Management for Natural Hazards, Working Paper, The Wharton School, University of Pennsylvania.

return on investment, the investor faces the possibility of losing either a portion or its entire principal investment. The amount paid out to the firm (i.e. the ceding company) depends on how the cat bond is constructed and this amount is specified in advance of the triggering event. Notably, the firm does not face any credit risk from the cat bond; the money to pay for the losses is already in hand. Many of the cat bonds being issued today are tied to a disaster-severity index (e.g., covering damage from a certain earthquake magnitude event within a specified region) rather than to the firm's actual losses. Since these parameters are normally independent of the firm's actual losses, payments can be made to the firm immediately after the disaster occurs rather than being subject to the time delay necessary to compute actual losses, as in the case of insurance or reinsurance.

Hence indexed cat bonds reduce the amount of moral hazard in loss estimation. On the other hand, such a cat bond creates *basis risk*. Basis risk refers to the imperfect correlation between the actual losses suffered by the firm and the payments received from the cat bond. Insurance sold to firms or excess-of-loss reinsurance to insurers has very little basis risk because there is a direct relationship between the loss and the payment delivered by the reinsurance instrument.

In May of 1999, a parametric-based contract to cover the loss from an earthquake was purchased by Oriental Land, a Japanese company that is best known as the owner and operator of Tokyo Disneyland. This cat bond provides $100 million to the company should an earthquake of a specific magnitude occur in the vicinity of Tokyo. The Japanese Meteorological Agency determines the measurement of event magnitude. The magnitude which qualifies a given quake for payments to Oriental Land is higher as the locations of its epicenter becomes more remote from Tokyo Disneyland. These bonds represent the first direct access of the capital markets by a corporation seeking catastrophe risk financing. An effective cat bond can benefit an insurer by reducing the effects of the lp-hc events in the right tail of the Loss EP curve. By paying the insurer only for lp-hc events, a cat bond basically reduces the right tail losses. Since total annual insurance premiums are collected based on a certain "loading factor", times annual expected losses from the hazard to the insurer, a reduction in the right tail reduces expected losses and hence reduces insurance premiums.

Because the high consequence events in the right tail occur with low robabilities, it is possible to cut right tail losses by a large amount while reducing expected losses by a relatively small amount. Consequently, insolvency probability would fall significantly for only a small decease in premiums. In this case, the annual profits to the insurer, defined as Profits = Total Premiums – Expected Losses + Payments to Insurer from CB – Price of CB, will also not suffer after the purchase of a reasonably priced cat bond.

The cat bonds are expensive risk transfer alternatives in today's market. Investors demand abnormally high returns on the bonds, making them costly relative to reinsurance. Hence an indexed cat bond must be well-parameterized with very little basis risk in order to be attractive to an insurer.

## Homeowners' Decision Processes and Strategies

In order to develop alternative risk management strategies for natural disasters, it is important to understand when homeowners voluntarily invest in a cost-effective risk mitigation measure (RMM). The definition of *cost-effective* in this paper is related solely to structural damage to the property. In other words, one determines whether the expected discounted benefits as measured by the reduction in damage to the house exceeds the cost of the mitigation measure. Those measures that meet this criterion will certainly be viewed as desirable when one takes into account other direct and indirect benefits to the property owner(s), such as saving lives, reducing injuries and the pleasure of not being forced to leave one's home after a disaster.

To illustrate, consider a standard RMM for earthquakes: reinforcing crippled walls and bolting a house to a foundation. Although the upfront expense normally runs from US $ 1,000 to US $ 3,000, it yields sufficient expected benefits to be cost-effective for many homes in earthquake prone areas in California. Yet in a 1989 survey of 3,500 homeowners in four California counties subject to earthquake damage, only between 5 and 9 percent of the respondents in each of these counties reported adopting this or any other earthquake mitigation measure (Palm *et. al.* 1990). A follow-up survey of residents affected by the October 1989 Loma Prieta earthquake and the Northridge earthquake of 1994 revealed that only 10 percent of homeowners invested in any type of structural loss-reduction measure whether or not they were affected by recent earthquakes in the State (Palm, 1995).

There are at least five reasons why homeowners do not appear to want to invest in cost-effective RMMs. They importance of these factors will vary across different regions and may change over time depending on the area's disaster history and the response from the public sector following the most recent event.

### (a) Short Time Horizons

Individuals may have relatively short time horizons over which they want to recoup their investment in a mitigation measure. Even if the expected life of the house is 25 or 30 years, the person may only look at the potential benefits from the measure over the next 3 to 5 years. They may reason that they will not be residing in the property for longer than this period of time and/or that they want a quick return on their investment.

### (b) High Discount Rates

The need for a quick return is also consistent with having a high discount rate regarding future payoffs. Loewenstein and Prelec (1992) propose a behavioural model of choice whereby the discount function is hyperbolic, rather than exponential. Their model appears to explain the reluctance of individuals to incur the high immediate cost of energy-efficient appliances in return for reduced electricity charges over time (Hausman, 1979; Kempton and Neiman, 1987).

### (c) Underestimation of Probability

Some individuals may perceive the probability of a disaster causing damage to their property as being sufficiently low that the investment in the protective measure will not be justified. For example they may relate their perceived probability of a disaster (p) to a threshold level (p*) below which they do not worry about the consequences at all. If they estimate $p < p^*$, then they assume that the event "will not happen to me" and take no protective actions

### (d) Aversion to Upfront Costs

If people have budget constraints then they will be averse to incurring the upfront costs associated with a protective measure simply because they feel they cannot afford it.

### (e) Truncated Loss Distribution

Individuals may have little interest in investing in protective measures if they believe that they will be financially responsible for only a small portion of their losses should a disaster occur. If their assets are relatively limited in relation to their estimated potential loss, then these individuals may feel they that they can walk away from their destroyed home without being financially responsible. Similarly, if residents anticipate liberal disaster relief from the government should they suffer damage, they would have less reason to invest in a cost effective mitigation measure.

## Tools of Disaster Management

There are several different strategies for reducing future losses from natural disasters and providing protection for victims of natural disasters that complement each other. These range from mitigation measures prior to a disaster, the use of warnings and evacuation plans to reduce loss of lives and damage at the onset of an event and recovery strategies such as insurance and financial assistance following a disaster. We presently examine three policy tools as part of a disaster management strategy: well-enforced building codes for mitigating losses, disaster insurance, indexed-based or parameterized cat bonds.

### *(i) Well-Enforced Building Codes*

Building codes mandate that property owners adopt mitigation measures. Such codes may be desirable when property owners would otherwise not adopt cost-effective RMMs because they either misperceive the benefits from adopting the measure and/or underestimate the probability of a disaster occurring. If a family is forced to vacate its property because of damage that would have been prevented if a building code had been in place, then this additional cost needs to taken into account by the public sector when evaluating the cost-effectiveness of an RMM from a societal perspective. Cohen and Noll (1981) provide an additional rationale for building codes. When a structure collapses it may create externalities in the form of economic dislocations that are beyond the physical damage suffered by the owners. These may not be taken into account when the owners evaluate the importance of adopting a specific mitigation measure. For example, if a building topples off its foundation after an earthquake, it could break a pipeline and cause a major fire that would damage other structures not affected by the earthquake in the first place. There are several key interested parties who can enforce building codes. Banks and financial institutions could require an inspection of the property to see that it meets code before issuing a mortgage. Similarly, insurers may want to limit coverage only to those structures that meet the building code. Inspecting the building to see that it meets code and then providing it with a seal of approval provides accurate information to the property owner on the condition of the house. It also signals to others that the structure is disaster-resistant. This new information could translate into higher property values if prospective buyers took the earthquake risk into consideration when making their purchase decisions.

### (ii) Disaster Insurance

Disaster insurance is an important policy tool in the developed world in dealing with the cost of natural disasters. The costs of natural disasters have increased for the developed world dramatically in the past decades as well. The increased concentration of populations and property values in the developed world, particularly the United States, has increased dramatically the economic costs of natural disasters to that part of the world. In the developed world, the economic costs of natural disasters have been spread through the use of risk transfer techniques. The most common tool for spreading the risk associated with natural disasters is excess of loss insurance coverage. This coverage spreads the risk of natural disaster loss to the world reinsurance community and through them to the world capital markets. During the past five years, the amount of coverage purchased by the developing countries of the world has increased by 31%. The amount of natural disaster reinsurance purchased is approximately 53 billion USD, or 50% more than the average annual damage of USD 35 billion caused by natural disasters in the developed world. Through the use of insurance and reinsurance, a substantial portion of the losses from natural disasters is borne by others than the victims and governments in those countries. In the United States, nearly 70% of the natural disaster losses from natural disasters are from hurricanes. In the United States, 85% of the losses to private property from hurricanes are insured. On average, the insurance industry absorbs 60% of the private property losses from natural disasters in the U.S.

While disaster insurance is fairly extensive in the United States—more than 50 percent of direct losses from natural disasters is insured—it is much less commonplace in other developed countries. In Austria, the Czech Republic, and Germany, for instance, only about 10–20 percent of the losses from the floods in 2002 were insured. And, in countries with per capita incomes below $10,000, insurance coverage is less than 10 percent; in those with per capita incomes under $760, it is about 1 percent. Asia, which suffered half of all the damage caused by natural disasters and two-thirds of all the casualties from catastrophic events in 1997, accounted for only 8 percent of global purchases of catastrophic insurance, whereas Japan, the United Kingdom, and the United States—less than 2 percent of the total market—accounted for 55 percent of the total.

In the developing world, almost no insurance and reinsurance exists to absorb the cost of natural disasters. Disaster insurance is largely confined to wealthy individuals and large enterprises, such as utilities and hotels, that are strongly affected by the weather. Such insurance schemes as have existed—usually offered by the public sector—have often failed because of high administrative costs, inefficient loss calculation, and inadequate premium charges. In many countries, governments have stifled the development of innovative insurance products by operating highly subsidized public insurance programs. There are important failures in the market for disaster insurance. Adverse selection—the purchaser of insurance knowing more about the underlying risk than the seller—may be less of a problem than in other insurance markets, in that the likelihood of disaster is, in principle, knowable with some accuracy, as is the value of the property at stake.

In Asia, less than 2% of the damage from natural disaster is insured As a result, nearly all the losses from floods in Asia are absorbed either by the governments or victims in those countries (Swiss Re, 1997). The lack of insurance for natural disaster is in contrast to the use of insurance in the developing world for other risks. The developing world is responsible for 14% of the worldwide direct insurance business, and almost 19% of the demand for non-life reinsurance. The use of insurance, and especially reinsurance, is therefore not unknown to these regions of the world. The failure of any effective market for natural disaster insurance has meant that the risk spreading benefits and costs of natural disaster insurance have bypassed the developing world.

### *(iii) Indexed Based or Parameterized Cat Bonds*

In contrast to an indemnity contract where the entity providing protection (e.g. the reinsurer) can become insolvent if it suffers catastrophic losses, the firm does not face any credit risk from an indexed based cat bond. The money to pay for the losses is already in hand. On the other hand, such a cat bond creates *basis risk*. Basis risk refers to the imperfect correlation between the actual losses suffered by the firm and the payments received from the cat bond. Insurance sold to firms or excess-of-loss reinsurance to insurers has zero basis risk because there is a direct relationship between the loss and the payment delivered by the reinsurance instrument.

## Natural Disaster Risk-Sharing: Implications for the Developing World

Risk transfer in the developed world is based on complex models of catastrophic risk exposure. During the past decade, these models have been essential for pricing and accumulating natural disaster risk. The outcomes of these models are compared to complex decision making models for both the sellers and buyers of risk to compare the benefit of risk transfer to its cost. In the developing world, the essential decision-making tools to evaluate alternative policy options are missing. Key among those tools is a clear understanding of the total impact of natural disasters.

In the developing world, the costs of natural disasters are borne by the victims and governments. When disaster occurs, governments currently generally rely on either reallocating domestic budgets, redirecting approved loans, aid and new loans to restore lost infrastructure. As long as the international community is willing to provide needed resources to the developing world, often at substantially reduced cost, to replace lost infrastructure, no change in current policy may be necessary. As the lending and aid community look at the options for more efficiently dealing with costs of natural disasters, the issue of risk transfer will become more important. In some cases, the use of risk transfer may be much more efficient than the use of *ex post* lending. Moreover, the equitable argument of allocating costs to activities may reduce the willingness of the international community to subsidize inefficient behavior. While risk transfer has proven to be an effective tool to deal with the costs of natural disasters in the developed world, its role in the developing world is still undefined.

## References

Arriens, W.T.L and Charlotte Benson (1999): "Post-Disaster Rehabilitation: The Experience of the Asian Development Bank", Paper before IDNR-ESCAP Regional Meeting for Asia: Risk Reduction and Society in the 21st Century, Bangkok, 23-26 February, 1999.

Bernknopf, Richard L., David S. Brookshire, and Mark A. Thayer (1990): "Earthquake and Volcano Hazard Notices: An Economic Evaluation of Changes in Risk Perceptions", *Journal of Environmental Economics and Management*, 18(1) : 35-49.

Barro, Robert J., and Xavier Sala-I-Martin, (1995): Economic Growth, New York, NY; McGraw-Hill Inc.

Born Patricia and W. Kip Viscusi (2006): The catastrophic effects of natural disasters on insurance markets, *Journal of Risk and Uncertainty*, (2006), 33:55–72

Brown, J.P. (1972): The Economic Effects of Floods, (Springer-Verlag: N.Y.).

Butler, James R. and Daniel, P. Doessel (1981): "Efficiency and Equity in Natural Disaster Relief," *Public Finance*, 36(2) :193-213.

Brookshire, David, S., Mark, A. Thayer, John Tschirhart, and William D. Schulze (1985): "A Test of the Expected Utility Model: Evidence From Earthquake Risks," *Journal of Political Economy*.

Cass, David (1965): "Optimum Growth in an Aggregative Model of Capital Accumulation," *Review of Economic Studies*, 32 (July): 233-40.

Congressional Budget Office (1992): "A Descriptive Analysis of Federal Relief, Insurance, and Loss Reduction Programs for Natural Hazards", Report to the Sub-committee on Policy Research and Insurance of the Committee of Banking, Finance, and Urban Affairs.

Cochrane, Harold (1974): "Predicting the Economic Impact of Earthquakes," in Harold C. Cochrane, J. Eugene Haas, Martin J. Bowden, and Robert W. Kates (eds), Social Science Perspectives on the Coming San Francisco Earthquake, Natural Hazards Research Paper, No. 25, Boulder: University of Colorado.

Cordes, Joseph J. and Anthony, M.J. Yezer (1998): "In Harm's Way: Does Federal Spending on Beach Enhancement and Protection Induce Excessive Development in Coastal Areas?" *Land Economics*, 74(1):128-45.

Cummins, J. David, and Helyette Geman (1995): "Pricing Catastrophe Insurance Futures and Call Spreads: An Arbitrage Approach, *Journal of Fixed Income*, 46-57.

Dacey, Douglas C. and Howard Kunreuther (1969): The Economics of Natural Disasters: Implications for Federal Policy, (New York: Free Press).

Ellison, Richard W., Jerome W. Milliman, and R. Blaine Roberts (1984):, "Measuring the Regional Economic Effects of Earthquakes and Earthquake Predictions," *Journal of Regional Science*, 24(4): 559-79.

Frame, David E., "Housing, Natural Hazards, and Insurance," *Journal of Urban Economics*, (1998), 44:93-109.

Guin Jayanta and Vinita Saxena (2007): "Extreme Losses From Natural Disasters—Earthquakes, Tropical Cyclones and Extratropical Cyclones", www.air-worldwide.com/_public/html/pubspc.asp.

Insurance Services Office (ISO) (1999): Financing Catastrophe Risk: Capital Market Solutions (New York, N.Y.: Insurance Services Office)

Hausman, Jerry (1979) "Individual Discount Rates and the Purchase and Utilization of Energy-Using Durables", *Bell Journal of Economics*, 10:33-54.

Jaffee, Dwight and Thomas Russel (1997) "Catastrophic Insurance, Capital Markets, and Uninsurable Risks," *Journal of Risk and Insurance*, (June 1997), pp 205-30.

Kleindorfer, P.R. and Kunreuther, H. (1999): "Challenges Facing the Insurance Industry in Managing Catastrophic Risks" in Kenneth Froot (ed.) *The Financing of Property/Casualty Risks* (Chicago: University of Chicago Press).

Koopmans, Tjalling C. (1965): "On the Concept of Optimal Economic Growth," in The Econometric Approach to Development Planning, Amsterdam, *The Netherlands*; North Holland.

Kreimer, Alcira *et al.* (1998): The World Bank's Experience with Post-Conflict Reconstruction, Washington D.C.: The World Bank.

Kunreuther, Howard (2001): Mitigation and Financial Risk Management for Natural Hazards, Working Paper, The Wharton School, University of Pennsylvania.

Kunreuther, Howard (1996): "Mitigating Disaster Losses through Insurance," *Journal of Risk and Uncertainty*, 171-87.

Kunreuther, Howard (1978): Disaster Insurance Protection: Public Policy Lessons. (John Wiley and Sons: New York).

Kunreuther, Howard, and Anne E. Kleffner (1992): "Should Earthquake Mitigation Measures Be Voluntary or Required?" *Journal of Regulatory Economics*, 321-33.

Kunreuther, Howard, Hogarth, Robin and Meszaros, Jacqueline, (1993): "Insurer Ambiguity and Market Failure," *Journal of Risk and Uncertainty*, 7: 71-87.

Kunreuther, Howard, and Richard Roth, Sr (editors).(1998): Paying The Price: The Status and Role of Insurance Against Natural Disasters in the United States, (Joseph Henry Press: Washington, D.C.).

Lewis, Christopher, and Kevin C. Murdock (1996): "The Role of Government Contracts in Discretionary Reinsurance Markets for Natural Disasters," *Journal of Risk and Insurance*, 567-97.

Lewis, Tracy, and David Nickerson (1989): "Self-Insurance Against Natural Disasters," *Journal of Environmental Economics and Management*, (1989), 16: 209-33.

Loewenstein George and Prelec, Drazen (1992): "Anomalies in Intertemporal Choice" Quarterly Journal of Economics, 107: 573-97.

Mayers, David, and Clifford Smith (1982). On corporate demand for insurance. *Journal of Business*, 55: 281-96.

Munich Re (1999): "Climate Change and Increase in Loss Trend Persist", Press Release, March 15, 1999.

Munich Re (1998b): "Munich Re's Review of Natural Catastrophes in 1998", Press Release, December 29, 1998.

Munich Re (1998a): World Map of Natural Hazards, Munich: Munich Re.

Munich Re (1998): Topics: Annual Review of Natural Catastrophes, 1997, Munich: Munich Re.

Okuyama, Yasuhide, Geoffrey J.D. Hewings, and Michael Sonis (1999): "Economic Impacts of an Unscheduled, Disruptive Event: A Miyazawa Multiplier Analysis," in Geoffrey J.D. Hewings, Michael Sonis, Moss Madden, and Yoshio Kimura (eds). "Understanding and Interpreting Economic Structures", New York, NY; Springer-Verlag: pp. 113-44.

Okuyama Yasuhide (2003): "Economics of Natural Disasters: A Critical Review", Paper presented at the 50th North American Meeting, *Regional Science Association International,* November 20-22, 2003, Philadelphia, PA.

Palm, Risa (1995): Earthquake Insurance: A Longitudinal Study of California Homeowners (Westview Press: Boulder, Colorado).

Palm, Risa, M. Hodgson, R. Blanchard, and D. Lyons (1990): "Earthquake Insurance in California," (Westview Press: Boulder, Colorado).

Ramsey, Frank (1928):"A Mathematical Theory of Saving," *Economic Journal,* 38 (December): 543-59.

Roy, A.D. (1952): "Safety-First and the Holding of Assets" *Econometrica,* 20: 431-49.

Rose, Adam, Juan Benavides, Stephanie E. Chang, Philip Szczesniak, and Dongsoon Lim (1997): "The Regional Economic Impact of an Earthquake: Direct and Indirect Effects of Electricity Lifeline Disruptions, *Journal of Regional Science,* 37(3): 437-58.

Rubin, Claire (1982): "Managing Recovery from a Natural Disaster." Management Information Service Representative, 14(2):1-15.

Scawthorn, Charles, Hirokazu Iemura, and Yoshikazu Yamada (1982): "The Influence of Natural Hazards on Urban Housing Location," *Journal of Urban Economics,* (March) 242-51.

Solow, Robert M. (1956): "A Contribution to the Theory of Economic Growth," *Quarterly Journal of Economics,* 70 (1): 65-94.

Shilling, James D., C.F. Sirmans, and John D. Benjamin (1989): "Flood Insurance, Wealth Redistribution, and Urban Property Values," *Journal of Urban Economics.*

Stone, James (1973): A theory of capacity and the insurance of catastrophe risks: Part I and Part II. *Journal of Risk and Insurance,* 40: 231-43 (Part I) and 40: 339-55 (Part II).

Swan, Trevor W. (1956): "Economic Growth and Capital Accumulation," *Economic Record,* 32 (November): 334-61.

Swiss Re (1999), Natural catastrophes and man-made disasters, 1998: Storms, hail and ice caused billion-dollar losses, sigma no. 1/1999, Zurich: Swiss Reinsurance Company.

Swiss Re (1998a): Floods—An Insurable Risk? Zurich: Swiss Reinsurance Company.

Swiss Re (1998b): Floods—An Insurable Risk? A Market Survey Zurich: Swiss Reinsurance Company.

Swiss Re (1997): Too little reinsurance of natural disasters in many markets, sigma no. 7/1997, Zurich: Swiss Reinsurance Company.

Swiss Re (1997a): Learning from Disaster: The floods in the Czech Republic, Poland and Germany in the summer of 1997, Zurich: Swiss Reinsurance Company.

Shinozuka, Howard and Richard J. Roth (ed.) (1998): Engineering and Socioeconomic Impacts of Earthquakes: An Analysis of Electricity Lifeline Disruptions in the New Madrid Area, New York: Multidisciplinary Center for Earthquake Engineering Research.

West, Carol T. and David G. Lenze (1994): "Modeling the Regional Impact of Natural Disaster and Recovery: A General Framework and Application to Hurricane Andrew," *International Regional Science Review,* 17(2):121-50.

The World Bank (1994): World Development Report, 1994: Infrastructure for Development, Washington D.C.: Oxford University Press.

The World Bank (1991): "World Development Report, 1990: Poverty", Washington D.C.: Oxford University Press.

Yezer, Anthony M.J. (1992): "Differential Impact of Earthquake Events" in *The Economic Consequences of a Catastrophic Earthquake*, National Academy of Sciences Press: Washington, D.C., pp. 112-18.

Yezer, Anthony M.J. and Claire B. Rubin (1987): "The Local Economic Effects of Natural Disasters, Working Paper #61, Institute of Behavioural Science, University of Colorado.

# Index